STRICTLY *Whitetails*

Tips, tales and techniques from a
white-tailed deer hunting expert

Written by Gary Clancy
Edited by Rob Drieslein
Art direction by Ron Nelson

Outdoor News, Inc.
New Hope, Minnesota

The Outdoor News Publications
3410 Winnetka Ave. N.
New Hope, MN 55427
(763) 546-4251
www.outdoornews.com

Strictly Whitetails
Tips, tales and techniques from a white-tailed deer hunting expert

Portions of this book originally appeared in *Outdoor News*.

Printed in the United States of America by Shakopee Valley Printing.

10 9 8 7 6 5 4 3 2 1

Cover images by Gary Clancy
Illustrations by Ron Nelson
Editorial Director: Rob Drieslein
Art Director: Ron Nelson

ISBN 0-9649257-6-1

To every hunter whose heart does a little dance at the mere sight of a gleaming rub, freshly pawed scrape, or a big, blunt-toed track in fresh snow.

Contents

Hunting tales

The offseason

Author's Acknowledgements

S trictly Whitetails the column spawned in 1999 out of my desire to share more about my favorite big game animal with you. My other column in *Outdoor News*, which has run weekly since 1992, under the banner "Enjoying Our Woods and Lakes," covers a broad spectrum of outdoor pursuits and interests. With all of the other activities I cover in that column, there simply was not space or time to do justice to the white-tailed deer. I suspected that there were enough of you who feel like I do about whitetails and that you would appreciate a column devoted specifically to the species.

I ran the idea for the column by Editor Rob Drieslein and Publisher Glenn Meyer, and they promptly gave me the thumbs-up. Of course, it did not take much selling on my part, since both Rob and Glenn are avid whitetail hunters.

From its inception, I have tried to write Strictly Whitetails as if you and I were sitting at the kitchen table talking about deer hunting over a cup of coffee. Although others may refer to me as an "expert whitetail hunter," you will not hear those words from these lips. Whatever an expert is, I am not one. I'm just a man who carries a never-ending and seemingly ever-increasing passion for the whitetail in his heart. Strictly Whitetails is my way of sharing that passion with you.

This book is not really my book. It's not Glenn's or Rob's or Ron's or the rest of the crew at *Outdoor News* who put their time and talents into it. This book belongs to you, the readers of *Outdoor News* who each week open your paper in the hope of finding a Strictly Whitetails column inside. Without you and your support, this book would never have happened.

I suspect that I will carry a copy of this book with me this fall as I travel to deer camps around the country. No, not to show off, or to sell. Instead, I will pull it out in the evenings as I sit by the fire letting the warmth from the flames flick away the chills and the stiffness that comes from sitting too long on stand, or from having climbed one too many hills. I'll read a few pages, then drift off to sleep and dream the dreams that, in November, are always strictly whitetails.

Hunt hard, shoot straight and be safe!

Gary Clancy
Feb. 10, 2002

FIELD SECRETS

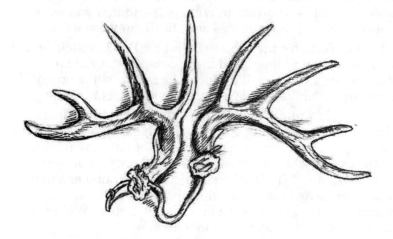

The art of still-hunting

Still-hunting today is a very effective, exciting, and rewarding style of hunting. But I fear that the art of still-hunting is being lost. What is not passed down usually disappears. Perhaps these few pages will encourage you to try still-hunting, then to pass on what you learn to a younger hunter.

Trying to instruct someone on how to still-hunt is like trying to explain to someone how to ride a bike — there are some things you just need to learn as you go. However, here are four concepts that will get you started:

• Force yourself to slow down. The world we live in places a premium on speed. Rush here, hurry there, grab a bite on the run, dash off to work, hurry to the woods to go hunting. A desire to do more, and do it faster, consumes our lives. Still-hunting crosses that notion.

Most hunters unsuccessful at still-hunting simply can't throttle down their internal engines to the idle best suited to still-hunting. I think that explains why fewer flags and more shootable deer appear as my season progresses. During the early days of the season I'm

The successful conclusion of a well-timed still-hunt will mark the high-point of your hunting career.

locked into that hurry-hurry mode, and the abundance of white flags mocking me in the distance reflects my condition.

As the season progresses, I become more in tune with the slower flow of life in the woods; I can sneak up on increasing numbers of deer unaware of my presence.

• Limit body motion. Most of us swagger, sway, and swing our arms when we walk down the street. All that extra motion in the woods will make you an easy mark for the whitetail's incredible ability to detect movement. Only your legs should be in motion when you step.

• When walking, put your foot down either heel or toe first, whichever is most comfortable for you, then let the rest of the foot roll slowly into place. By doing this you can feel most sticks beneath your feet before they crack.

• Pre-plan your next series of steps each time you stop. Look ahead 20 to 30 feet (never move farther than that between stops) and plan your route. Take advantage of game trails, old roads, creek beds, fallen trees, patches of bare earth, and anything else that will help you move as quietly as possible. Plan detours around patches of crusty snow, thick beds of sun-dried leaves, heavy brush and deadfalls. Purposefully plan each stop next to a tree, deadfall or bush; this will break up your outline and provide a steady rest for your rifle if a shot presents itself.

If you ever visit my home, you may notice a shoulder mount of a whitetail buck in the corner of my den. There is nothing extraordinary about the 10-point rack. But each time I look at the mount of that not-so-big-10-point, I remember the way the woods smelled on that rainy November morning. I can hear the patter of rain drops on already soggy leaves; I feel his eyes locking onto mine as he caught me in midstride, and the rush of relief I had when he dropped his head and returned to searching for acorns beneath the sopping forest duff.

I took him by still-hunting, and to me, that — more than sheer size — makes him a trophy.

A game plan for the archery opener

When Tiger Woods tees up that little white ball on the first day of any tournament, you can bet that he has a game plan for that day. My opening day game plan might not be worth a million bucks like Tiger's, but it is just as important to me. Without a game plan, my opening days are usually unproductive and disappointing. So for what it's worth, here is my annual opening day game plan for the whitetail archery season.

Since the archery deer season often opens in Minnesota and in Wisconsin on the same day, I make pre-season preparations in both states. Which state I hunt on Saturday will depend upon what my last-minute scouting on Friday reveals and what the wind directions are on the opener. I usually don't finalize my game plan until Friday night.

There have been many opening days when I did not hunt the first morning. I sometimes forego that first morning to avoid disturbing the deer I intend to hunt that evening. If there is any

Between the moderate temperatures, the relatively unpressured deer, and long autumn days, early season bowhunting provides one of the most gratifying forms of deer hunting in the Upper Midwest.

chance that my morning hunt will disrupt my evening, I'll scrap the morning hunt.

Evening is prime time in the early part of the season, and if you do not have a place to hunt without disturbing the same deer that you plan to hunt in the evening, wait until evening. The past few years, I've been fortunate to have two prime morning locations.

One is an oak flat between the soybean and alfalfa fields where the deer munch away the night hours and the ridge where many of them lie for the day. When the acorns are falling heavy and early, the deer will often stop to scarf up acorns before turning in for the day.

The other stand is located near a secluded little pond near a bedding area. Deer will drink before bedding down for the day, and by the looks of the tracks in the mud, this watering hole is mighty popular.

The oak flat will work with any wind out of the north or northwest. I hang two stands near the pond, so that I can hunt it regardless of wind direction. Depending upon the temperature, I'll usually sit there until 9:30 or so, then call it good until evening. Deer don't move much during the middle of the day during the heat of early archery.

For the evening hunt the past few years, I've had four options prepared. Two are on the edges of soybean fields that the deer really hammer late in the summer. These stands are always a little risky because when the soybeans mature or get nipped by a frost, the deer switch to alfalfa, natural browse, and acorns. If, however, the deer are still on the soybeans when opener arrives, these stands are as close to a sure-thing as you can get in the world of white-tailing.

One of the stands is located right at the corner where timber, standing corn, and soybeans all come together. This gives the deer lots of edges, but more importantly it allows me to hunt close to the corn. Many deer bed down in the corn at this time of the year, then saunter into the beans in the evening to chow down.

The other stand is set 25 yards from a trail deer use to access the field. Last year, one of the deer was a Pope and Young class 8-point. The other two options are the morning stands. Either will work well for an evening stand as well.

If I hunt either of the field edges, my wife, Nancy, picks me up at dark. When she drives near the field, the deer will spook off the field and give me time to get down out of my stand and bail out without ruining the field for another evening. The deer are accustomed to vehicles, and they will be back in the field before our taillights are out of sight.

For a typical opening day, my equipment is ready to go a week ahead of time. My turkey vest, which I use in place of a day pack or fanny pack, holds the rest of my essentials, such as binoculars, rangefinder, licenses, clipper, pull-up rope, and knife.

Make a game plan for opening day, and then, no matter what happens, remember: Bowhunting is not as serious as many of us make it. Have fun out there!

Sure-fire deer calling tactics

E very bowhunter I know (and most gun hunters) carry a grunt call into the woods, but only a small percentage of deer hunters have ever called in a deer. The main reason for this is that opening weekend of the firearms season is when the highest percentage of hunters with grunt calls strung around their neck are in the woods, and opening weekend of the firearms season is the worst time to call deer. Look at it this way: If someone was shooting at you, would you take time to answer the phone?

Forget about calling deer during significant hunting pressure. That does not mean that you cannot call in a deer on opening day or any time during the firearms season. Twice I've found myself hunting virtually alone on opening day of the firearms season, and if you're lucky enough to have the same experience, a grunt call can be a deadly tool.

When hunting with a shotgun, rifle, or muzzleloader, I consider the grunt call most effective in heavy cover where my visibility is limited. A few grunts or doe bleats might just bring a buck out of the brush where I can get a crack at him. In more open terrain, a grunt call is of less value, because you can see farther than a deer can hear the call. However, on a couple of occasions I've used a grunt call to get the attention of a buck that was out of range of my muzzleloader. One buck just stopped and stared and then continued to wherever he was headed, but the other made a fatal mistake and made a hard right turn to investigate the grunts. In my experience, that's about the results you can expect with a grunt call. Half of the bucks that hear it will respond, the other half will not, though the ratio improves when the rut is in progress.

I've lost count of the number of bucks that have responded to my calling while bowhunting — dozens of them anyway. Some I shot, most I let walk, but all were exciting. Any time an animal comes to the call, whether it's a coyote racing to a dying rabbit, a honker gliding into the decoys, a red-eyed bull elk challenging my bugle, or a buck slipping in to investigate my grunts, it's exciting, heart-pumping stuff. For bowhunters, I consider the grunt call an invaluable tool.

When I first began using a grunt call 20 years ago, I used it only on deer I could see. This was a good education, because when you call to a buck in sight, you can see how the deer reacts to various cadences and volume. After I had called in a few bucks with the grunt tube, I gained confidence and began to "call blind," which just means that I would send out a few grunts, even when there were no deer in sight. I have no way of estimating how many more bucks I saw because of calling blind; I cannot prove that I would not have seen those same bucks even if I had not been calling. But I believe that calling blind probably accounts for around 20 percent of my buck sightings in a year.

The thicker the cover, the more I call. My theory is simple. Let's say that I'm sitting in a treestand and can see pretty decent about 50 yards in all directions. Any deer within that 50 yards I should see or hear. But on a calm day, a buck can easily hear a grunt call a couple of hundred yards away. If I cut loose with a series of grunts every 15 minutes or so, there's a good chance those grunts will reach the ears of a buck within hearing distance of the call but not within my 50-yard zone. Simple math.

Calling works from opening day right up until the last bell, and I've personally called in bucks in the Midwest

The author believes every archery deer hunter should have a grunt tube strung around his or her neck before heading afield. Calling, Clancy maintains, works from opening day, during the rut, and through the end of the season.

during September, October, November, December, and January. Calling works best during the rut. From the time the bucks begin rubbing and scraping right up until the last doe has been bred, a buck is a sucker for a buck grunt or a doe bleat.

It makes sense. A buck only has one thing on his mind during the rut, and when he hears another buck grunt, odds are excellent he will determine if that buck has a doe with him. Over the years, while calling to bucks that I could see while the rut was in progress, I have had at least 75 percent of those bucks come to the call. Some of the bucks that did not respond were already trailing or tending a doe. It is not impossible to call a buck away from a doe, but it's very difficult.

The whitetail deer has 20-some different vocalizations to communicate with other deer. Luckily, you and I do not need to learn the entire language. The contact grunt, the tending grunt, and the doe bleat are all you really need. Today, thanks to the availability of variable-tone deer calls, you can make all three on the same call.

Not all deer calls are created equal. Some sound more like recycled duck calls, others are too tinny, and others require too much air pressure to activate. Some variable-tone calls require that you take the call apart and adjust a rubber band on the reed to change from a buck grunt to a doe bleat. Some of these calls sound great, but I like a call that can change pitch, volume, and sound without me taking my eye off the deer.

Whatever brand of call you own or purchase, obtain an instructional tape to go with it, then duplicate what you hear. And if you've never been too handy with a turkey call or duck call, don't let that stop you. Learning to vocalize on a good grunt tube is child's play by comparison.

I use the contact grunt early and late in the season before and after the rut. During the rut, I use the tending/trailing grunt and often mix in a few doe bleats to give the impression that there's a buck with a doe.

Reading early season buck rubs

If you're looking for a mature whitetail buck, next to actually laying eyes on the animal itself, the best proof you can find of a big buck's existence are its rubs. When I'm looking at a new hunting area and trying to determine the potential of that area for mature bucks (animals three years and older), I try to spend as much time as I can scouting and looking for rubs between mid-September and mid-October.

Why that one month span? Because it is during this period that mature bucks are busy making rubs. When you find rubs

during this period, especially rubs found anytime in September, odds are excellent that a mature buck made them. From mid-October on, the young bucks get into action rubbing, and since there are far more 1- and 2-year-old bucks in the population than there are mature bucks, rubs pop up everywhere.

When all of the bucks are making rubs, it's difficult to sort out those made by small bucks and those made by the big guys. Sometimes the size of the sapling being

Find a rub in late September and early October, and you can bet that a large buck has left its mark. Later, smaller bucks get in on the rubbing action.

rubbed indicates the age of the buck that made the rub, but not always. While it is true that only mature deer rub trees six inches or more in diameter, it is also true that the same monster buck that will rub a cedar fencepost in half (I've seen it), will display his handiwork on spindly saplings no bigger around than a good cigar. So while you can't write off all small rubs as being made by immature bucks only, you can bet that when you run across a nasty rub on a tree the size of a pulling guard's biceps, that you're looking at a rub made by a dominant buck.

While giving seminars, I often hear hunters complain that the bucks in the area they hunt just don't start rubbing until mid to late October. Although these hunters spend a lot of time looking in mid and late September, they fail to find rubs. I hate to be the one to break the bad news to them, but the reason for this, if they have made a thorough search, is that there are no mature bucks in the area they are hunting. Unfortunately, this is not uncommon. Many areas have few if any mature bucks in the population.

I have heard it argued that if an area lacks bucks that are three years or older to fill the dominant buck role, those two- and even one-year-old bucks will fill the vacant slot. Though it's true that these younger bucks will breed when the rut kicks in, these younger deer don't begin to rub any earlier just because they're now the biggest boys on the block. Nature doesn't work that way.

Rubs, at least those made by mature bucks, are not made by bucks trying to rid their antlers of velvet, and they are not merely sparring partners for strengthening neck muscles. When a mature buck makes a rub, he is leaving behind a visual signal of his presence and his dominance, but more importantly, the buck leaves behind a secretion from his forehead gland on each rub he makes. This scent tells other deer where the buck ranks in the social order. Researchers have recently discovered that the scent left behind on rubs by mature bucks tends to suppress the urge to breed in younger bucks, and at the same time helps to sexually stimulate the does.

Talk about a double-whammy: Turn off the competition while you turn on the object of your desire!

Rattlin'

P rime time for rattling action occurs from Oct. 20 through Thanksgiving. However, once gun seasons kick in and the woods fill with hunters, rattling success decreases while hunting pressure remains a dominant factor.

Now, that does not mean you cannot rattle in a buck during a gun season. I've done it and so have others. In fact, I once rattled in and killed a fine 8-point buck on Minnesota's opening morning. That doesn't happen often. But on that frosty November morning, there were no other hunters on the farm I hunted, conditions were ideal for rattling, and I figured I'd give it a try. The hunch paid off.

Lots of hunters don't believe that rattling will work in farm country, but that's not true. Rattling will work anywhere. I've rattled in bucks in Minnesota, Wisconsin, Michigan, South Dakota, Iowa, Montana, Illinois, Kansas, Missouri, Georgia, Nebraska, Texas, Saskatchewan and Alberta. Rattling is more productive in some of those places than others, but rattling will work on whitetails anywhere.

Bucks are most

Be patient when rattling deer. Any form of game calling will be more unsuccessful than successful, but when it pays off, you can't beat the rush!

responsive to rattling in areas where the buck-to-doe ratio is not heavily slanted in favor of the females. Competition between bucks for the available does makes for really good rattling action. Another factor that influences your success is the number of mature bucks in the population. The more bucks at least 3½ years old, the more response you will have with the antlers.

Most hunters give up on rattling too easy. Any time you're calling game, you are going to be unsuccessful more than you are successful. Even in Texas, where rattling is more effective than anywhere I have hunted, few deer come to the horns.

If I'm hunting from a treestand, I'll usually shake the antlers every hour. If I'm hunting terrain or cover where I can't see very far, I'll increase the frequency. After all, the whole idea behind rattling is to draw bucks that you otherwise probably would not have seen.

I start out with a few grunts and bleats on my grunt call. I'll wait a minute or so to see if any deer come to the call, then I'll begin rattling.

I'll rattle for a long time, usually at least four or five minutes, sometimes twice that long. Every 30 seconds or so I stop to listen for any deer approaching. Most of the bucks I've rattled in have come in a hurry, but I've had them show up near the end of a long rattling session with their mouths open and breathing hard, which indicates they will sometimes come a long way to the sound of clattering antlers.

My favorite instruments when rattling are a set of real antlers. I once had a dandy set of about 135-inch heavy horns, but someone stole them from me at a seminar. I don't think you need antlers that heavy, but they felt great in my hands and I had rattled in a bunch of bucks with them. I know that they were nothing but old bone, but doggone it, I miss those horns!

Even though I prefer real antlers, I don't think you'll rattle in any more bucks with real antlers than with synthetic antlers, a rattling bag, or any other rattling device. When a buck is ready to come to the horns, you can entice him by clattering a couple of arrows together (which has worked for me a time or two.)

My fanny pack or turkey vest always has a rattling bag in it. Many times when I hunt for the day, I don't plan to rattle much, so I don't bother toting along my rattlin' horns. On countless times on these days, I will decide to rattle a little or spot a buck out of range and get his attention. That is where the rattling bag comes into play. My biggest buck in 2000, a dandy 15-pointer, came running to a rattling bag.

Many hunters are reluctant to rattle because they think it will scare off more bucks than it will attract. I don't think rattling scares deer often. Occasionally I've spooked deer that were close when I began rattling, deer that I should have seen before I ever brought the horns together. But at a distance, I doubt rattling scares deer. After all, they hear it all the time.

Rattling is no gimmick. It works. Commit yourself to rattling in a buck and stick with it. One day a buck will come charging into the horns and then, like me, you will be hooked on rattling for life. Happy horn-shaking!

Opening weekend pressure plays

When the annual firearms deer season opens, the single most important factor dictating success is not how well traveled the trail in front of your stand might be, the size of the scrapes, the number of rubs, the thickness of the bedding area, or how plentiful the food supply.

Under normal conditions, all of these "signs" would be important, but there is nothing normal about opening weekend. Unless you're fortunate enough to hunt your own property, there are few places in the Upper Midwest where hunting pressure will not be the main catalyst for deer movement on the opening weekend of the deer season.

Sure, you must consider the rut, but usually hunting pressure during the first couple of days of the season is intense enough that most bucks put survival ahead of sex, at least during the daylight hours. For this column, let's concentrate on hunting pressure and how you can let those other hunters work for you.

Forget the rut on the opening weekend of your state's firearms season. Hunting pressure becomes the dominant factor when hordes of orange-clad hunters appear, and you must alter your whitetailing tactics appropriately.

There is a very simple rule I follow any time hunting pressure is a factor in deer movement. One, I determine where the pressure will originate (Point A), and two, determine where the deer will head once the guns start barking (Point B). If you know of a Point A and a Point B where you hunt, you're in business. If not, get yourself an aerial photograph of the area. With such a photograph, you can pick out all the potential point As and Bs in your hunting area. In fact, even if you have hunted the same area for years, you will find an aerial photograph an invaluable tool.

Once you have this information, decide whether to position yourself between Point A and Point B, or take a stand within the escape cover itself, which is Point B. I let my familiarity with the land or an aerial photograph help with this decision. If there is a natural or man-made funnel somewhere along the route the deer likely will take as they move from the source of the most intense hunting pressure to the escape cover, my stand will overlook this pinch-point.

Any place that restricts lateral deer movement is a funnel, and there is no better place to sit on opening morning.

Common funnels are a narrow strip of high ground between lakes or sloughs, a fenceline connecting two woodlots, a place where the woods along a creek narrows to only 100 yards, or — in the hill country of southeast Minnesota or western Wisconsin — perhaps a sheer limestone bluff on one side and a river on the other with a flat, 50-yard wide swath of timber between the two. You get the idea.

If you cannot find a funnel, then set up on the edge of the escape cover or within the escape cover itself. Most of the time, the escape cover will be the thickest, nastiest cover in the area.

Look for ground cover that hunters walk around instead of through. If it is wet, all the better. Old deer have found refuge in these places before. The old deer introduce the young deer to these places. Consequently, good escape cover is used by deer year after year. The deer simply crawl into these hell holes and stay put until dark.

I'll warn you, hunting these places is not much fun. If the place is worth hunting, you won't see as far as Brett Favre can toss a football. With shots ringing out all around you, staying put on a stand in one of these thick places becomes a real mind game. My brain always screams to abandon ship and get out there in the open woods where I can see something. And I'll admit: I have spent all day on stand in these nasty places and not seen a single deer. But more often than not, hunting the places other hunters avoid pays dividends.

Besides being in the right place, you need to be there at the right time. Since I have no way of knowing if a buck is going to show at dawn, high noon, or just before the end of shooting hours, I just hunt all day. Lots of hunters claim to hunt all day, but few do. Most climb down from their stands or get up from their stump seat and go for a little warm-up walk, to check on their buddies, meet for lunch, or help Joe drag out his buck.

Maybe they'll put on a drive or two with friends. All of that activity keeps deer on the move, and any time deer are on the move, the best place to be is on stand overlooking a high travel area. Sounds simple, but it's not. Staying put all day on stand, no matter how good the stand, is tough. Few hunters can pull it off, but those who do rarely fail to use their tag.

Into the stand before first light and down when shooting hours are over. Some call it boring. I call it deadly.

Making the shot

Funny thing about deer hunting. Some of the guys and gals who are the best shots, those shooters who can put one hole right on top of another at the range, often blow a lot of opportunities in the deer woods. Then again, mediocre shots always seem to bring home the venison when they hunt. What gives? It has to do with several often overlooked, but vitally important points.

•Forget the perfect shot. You know, like the one you see in all of the pretty pictures in magazines, where the monster buck poses broadside a stone's throw away and looks the other way. In the real world of deer hunting, always take the first good shot available. I wish I had a $5 bill for each time I have heard

In open country, a pair of shooting sticks can help steady your rifle for those long-range opportunities.

this sad story:

"I had a good opportunity for the shot at about 75 yards, but he was coming my way, so I figured I would let him come right into that opening in front of my stand and I would have a 30-yard broadside shot. But something spooked him, maybe my scent, I don't know, but he was gone."

•I know it sounds silly, but humor me, all right? Get dressed in all of your hunting clothes and then practice mounting your rifle, shotgun, or muzzleloader to shoulder. Do it sitting, kneeling, and standing. Does the butt of the stock catch or hang-up on your clothing anywhere? If it does, now is the time to fix the problem.

•Sure the rifle was dead-on when you put it away after last season. And yes, it should be dead-on again this year. But if not? I've had rifles off as much as eight inches after sitting in the gun closet for a year. How does it happen? I don't have a clue. But it happens and the time to find out is before the season, not after you miss, or worse yet, wound a deer.

•While you are watching Monday Night Football or Inside Baseball, lay your rifle in your lap and practice slipping the safety off or cocking the hammer. Practice until you can do it without making a sound. Many a buck owes its life to the *click* of a safety or a hammer being locked back.

•Take off that sling and put it in your daypack. Slings get in the way when hunting. They hang up on brush and bramble at bad times. Slings also give you an excuse for hanging that rifle over your shoulder when hiking through the woods instead of having it in your hands when a buck bolts from nearby cover. When the hunt is over and you're dragging out your deer, then you can sling your rifle.

•Most shots at moving deer are not necessary. Unless a deer is really spooked, it will stop if you grunt, whistle, or even holler at it. Just have the deer in your sights before you do any of the three, because the deer will not stop for long.

•Always use a rest. Few of us shoot enough to be accurate from the unstable off-hand position. Usually there's time to find a limb, tree trunk, or stump to serve as a rest, but I always carry shooting sticks with me just in case.

•If a deer drops in its tracks when you fire, watch that deer closely. If it moves, even a twitching ear, shoot it again. If you drop a deer in its tracks but cannot see it from your stand, get to the deer quickly. Often a shot near the spine is enough to knock a deer off its feet — momentarily paralyzing it — but it will soon regain its senses and run away.

I remember a monster of a Saskatchewan buck that I rattled in, but he caught me with the rattling horns in my hands. We saw each other at the same instant. I flung the antlers to the ground while the buck went slinking away through some thick willow shoots rimming the bank of the dried-up slough by my stand. I shot and the buck went down.

Instinctively, I reloaded my muzzleloader as fast as I could. I had just put a fresh cap on the nipple when the buck, motionless during the 30 seconds or so it took me to reload the rifle, bounced to his feet and blasted off through the willows. I got lucky with the second shot and broke his neck.

Luck. You make your own ... every time.

Ten firearms deer season commandments

When the firearms deer season opens, every hunter hitting the woods is filled with anticipation and shared excitement. Eight hours later, many of those same hunters will be disillusioned. By Sunday night, half of them head for home with another unpunched tag in their pocket.

Of course luck plays a part in any hunt and nobody, no matter how good, is going to be successful all of the time. But follow these 10 commandments of deer hunting and I will guarantee that you will see more deer, have more opportunities for good shots, and have more fun hunting.

I — *Thou shalt sight-in from the bench but practice off-hand, kneeling, and sitting.*

There are no shooting benches in the deer woods. After sighting in from the bench, hang 8-inch paper plates on the backstop at the range and practice shooting at them from the ranges and positions you'll use in the woods. I hear hunters bragging all of the time about one-inch groups off the bench and then the same hunters can't smack a 250-pound buck in the boilers at 50 yards when faced with an in-the-woods shooting situation.

II — *Thou shalt look for sign of a hit after every shot.*

I was sitting on a bluff overlooking a valley in the Whitewater Wildlife Management Area one opening day of the deer season, when I saw two hunters emerge from the woods and start walking down a trail along a strip-picked cornfield. Just then, another hunter emerged from a gully and spooked three deer that ran across the cornfield toward the two hunters. They heard the deer and got into kneeling positions. When the three deer broke from the corn, they were about 50 yards from the two hunters. All three deer skidded to a halt and stared at the two orange blobs.

The hunters fired a volley of shots and one of the deer dropped in its tracks. One of the other deer raced for the woods and the other whirled and ran back into the corn. I quickly lost track of the deer that ran into the timber, but I could easily follow the retreat of the deer in the corn from my elevated vantage point. The deer in the corn ran about 100 yards and then pitched over dead. The two hunters hammered away until the deer were out of sight, then they walked to the fallen deer, field dressed it and began dragging it down the trail. They never looked for any sign of a hit from either of the other two deer. I climbed down from the bluff and intercepted the two hunters as they dragged the deer from the woods. I told them what I had seen and took them back to where the other deer lay dead in the corn. The shot had been perfect, broadside through both lungs, but because the deer had not stumbled, fallen, or shown any sign of a hit, the two hunters assumed they had missed. Never assume. Always look.

III — *Thou shalt attempt to stop a moving deer before shooting.*

A stationary target is easier to hit than a moving target. Unless a deer is really spooked, you can usually get it stop long enough to offer you a good shot. A walking deer will stop if you grunt or whistle softly. On a running deer, use a loud whistle or holler.

IV — *Thou shalt sit quietly in one spot for at least four hours.*

Most of the deer that are killed during the first few days of the season are deer that are on the move as they try to evade other hunters. If you sit still in a good spot (or even a not-so-good location) your odds of getting a shot at one of these deer is excellent. If you convince yourself that you should be hunting on the other side of the hill, or that you should check up on your buddies to see how they are doing, you become one of the reasons deer are on the move.

V — *Thou shall not make any quick movement.*

You have better eyesight than a white-tailed deer, so how come they

A treestand allows you to see deer from a greater distance, and deer also are less likely to spot you.

so often spot you first? Movement. A whitetail is a master at detecting motion. Do everything in slow motion on stand. Move only your eyes when scanning, not your head. When you must move your head, do it slowly.

VI — *Thou shalt use binoculars.*

Yep — even those of you hunt in shotgun-only zones — use binoculars, and you'll see more deer before they see you. It's that simple.

VII — *Thou shalt not give up at mid-morning.*

By mid-morning and certainly by noon, if a hunter has not scored, he is on the move. He might be attempting to still-hunt, checking on his partners, or hiking back to the truck or camp for lunch. All that movement stirs up deer. Stay put and you'll be in position to take advantage of it. I've killed a bunch of deer between 10 a.m. and 2 p.m.

VIII — *Thou shalt not get cold.*

OK, so you are going to get cold, but hey, you don't have to get so cold that you abandon your stand. Back when the best we could do was cotton longjohns and newspapers stuffed in over-shoes for insulation, staying on stand was torture. But today, with excellent boots, wool, polypropylene, and fleece clothing insulated with wonder fibers and disposable handwarmers for extra heat, there is no excuse for letting the cold beat you.

IX — *Thou shalt hunt until the last legal minute.*

I would be willing to bet that not one out of 10 hunters is still on stand during the last minutes of shooting light and that half of those hunters still on stand are not in their prime locations, but rather watching a trail closer to camp or vehicle. But the last minutes of shooting light are magical times for whitetails. Not only is this the natural time for the whitetail to begin stirring, but with the sudden lack of hunter activity, even the bigger bucks feel safe moving about. Carry a compass, a GPS if you have one, and two flashlights. You'll be more inclined to stick it out to the final bell.

X — *Thou shalt hunt high and wear a safety belt.*

Hunting from a treestand has many advantages. Not only can you usually spot deer at a greater distance from a tree than you can from the ground, but deer are less likely to see you, hear you, or smell you when you hunt from a treestand. And please, always wear a safety harness.

It ain't over 'til it's over

Funny thing about deer hunters. Whether you're talking about deer hunters in Minnesota, Packer country lads in Wisconsin, or whitetail aficionados in Michigan, after the first couple of days of the season, most deer hunters give up. Many go home. Some stay and hunt another day or two, but their hearts are not really in it. They don't believe they'll see much. And of course, with that attitude, they don't.

Statistics are part of the problem. A look at the numbers will reveal that 60, 70, and sometimes 80 percent of the harvest occurs on opening weekend of the firearms season. Big deal. Those numbers don't mean that 80 percent of the deer are dead and hanging in a locker or from a meat pole at someone else's camp. There are still plenty of deer in the woods after the opening weekend festivities. You just need to use different tactics than on opening weekend.

Why shouldn't you give up after opening weekend? Because, the author says, quite often the rut is on, and with most hunters out of the woods, opportunities for big, relatively unpressured bucks abound.

On the opener, you can depend upon hunting pressure to keep deer on the move. That's why so many of them die. They blunder into you while trying to evade me, or vice versa. But after opening weekend, hunting pressure is no longer a major factor. So now what?

In Minnesota, another major player works in our favor. We humans call it the rut. Take the autumn of 2000, when buck movement from Halloween through opening weekend was frantic. Most of the bucks I saw while bowhunting in Minnesota and Wisconsin during this period, and while gun hunting in Minnesota on the weekend, were looking for does. I saw two bucks, both of them big boys that already had found willing does and were sticking close.

Early November is prime time for bucks. Sure, hunting pressure puts a damper on the annual festivities, but not for long. Once the majority of hunters are out of the woods, it's back to business as usual for Mr. and Mrs. Whitetail. As long as bucks are on the prowl for does or even in the company of receptive does, your odds of encountering a buck after opening weekend are excellent.

Many gun hunters scoff at using scents, grunt calls, or rattling devices, considering them ineffective during the firearms season, and in the case of calling and rattling, far more likely to bring in a hunter than a buck. My experiences have been positive with all three during the gun season. I carry a rattling bag in my fanny pack and a Tru-Talker grunt tube around my neck no matter if I am hunting with a gun or bow. I don't use them if there are other hunters around, but very often I've had the woods all to myself later in the season.

Deer scents work. They don't work all of the time (nothing does) and they won't make up for sloppy hunting, but I've had a lot of positive results from deer scents. I usually lay down a scent trail of doe-in-estrus to my stand. You can use a commercial applicator or make one by using a clean rag tied to a piece of twine. Apply scent and drag it behind you as you hike to your stand. If a buck crosses the trail, he might put his nose to it and follow it right to you. I've had it happen many times. In fact, my biggest buck died this way.

When I get to my stand, I hang a few scent wicks with doe-in-estrus lure. These do three things. One, as the scent drifts downwind, it may attract the attention of a buck and bring him within range. Second, the smell of the urine helps cover my human odor. And third, I've seen many bucks stop at a scent wick to investigate the smell. That makes for an easy shot.

But even if you do not use scents, rattle, or call, as long as the rut is still on there is always a chance. Try to focus on the places where you usually see does. That may mean hunting the ridges and thickets where does bed in the morning and at midday and then hunting nearer the food source for the evening. Or maybe you know of a good funnel. There is no better place to park yourself.

If conditions are right, I sneak along slowly, stopping often to look and listen, then taking a few more cautious steps. Wet leaves — or better yet, a fresh snow — are ideal for this type of hunting.

When the rut is on, if you jump or see a doe, stay ready. Many times when tending a doe, the buck will lie down and eye the doe from his bed. The buck almost always watches the doe and not you. Often times I've had them get up when the doe bolts and look around to see what spooked her. If you're ready, you'll get a shot.

Hunting later in the season may not be as exciting as the first couple of days. The anticipation level is lower, and it's easy to convince yourself that it is a hopeless cause. But if you stick with it and hunt smart, you will taste the satisfaction that comes with hanging your tag on a deer after most hunters have called it quits.

Hunting the rut after opener

A fter the first three days of firearms hunting in most Midwestern states, you'll see a noticeable decline in the number of hunters. Deer notice, too. White-tailed deer react quickly to a sudden influx of hunters, but they also quickly respond to a dramatic decrease in hunting pressure.

In states and provinces where the gun season doesn't coincide with the rut, the whitetail's response to a decrease in hunting pressure is less noticeable than in Minnesota.

Not that white-tailed deer will quit rutting when the firearms season opens. Many bucks fall on opening weekend because they can't get their mind off sex long enough to concentrate on survival. No, the rut doesn't screech to a halt when the Minnesota firearms season opens, but the opening weekend of the season definitely dampens the once-a-year activity of procreating the species. Most of the hanky-panky occurs on Saturday and Sunday night, while they spend daylight hours avoiding all of us hunters.

But when the hunters leave,

Deer often return to business as usual when hunting pressure drops after the opening weekend of firearms deer season. Keep hunting and you may score big.

the whitetail resumes business as usual, and since the days following opening weekend will find the bulk of the does entering estrus, these are busy, busy times for whitetails. There will be a lot of trailing and tending, and with the absence of hunters, much of this activity will occur in broad daylight. Here's how to make sure you don't miss out on the action when the rut resumes.

•Pack a lunch and stay in the woods all day. At this time of the year, the hours from 11 a.m. to 2 p.m. produce a tremendous number of buck sightings for me. It's no coincidence that these are the same hours that other hunters vacate the woods for a midday break.

•Those same thickets you hunted the first few days of the season are not a bad choice, but there are better places to hunt now that bucks are moving rather than hiding out. Funnels are my first choice — a narrow strip of timber with water on two sides, a brushy fenceline connecting two woodlots, a gate or low spot in a fence. There are dozens of other examples of funnels, but all have one thing in common — they restrict lateral movement.

•In hill country, you can't beat a saddle on a steep ridge. Bucks, especially the big boys, always take the easy way, and a saddle provides the easiest route to move from one side of a ridge to another.

•If you know where does hang out during the day, hunt there in the morning. If you know where does feed in the evening, hunt near there in the afternoon.

•Use a doe-in-estrus scent. I don't know if the stuff actually comes from a doe in heat or not, but I know that it has worked wonders for me on many occasions. Put some on a clean rag and drag it behind you when you hike to your stand. Add more to the rag every 50 yards so that the scent builds as you approach your stand. Then hang the rag and three or four scent wicks dipped in scent in a circle around your stand. Not only are bucks attracted to the smell, but the odor from the scent wicks covers your human odor.

•Use a grunt call and rattling antlers. No, you probably won't pull a buck away from a hot doe, but remember, not every buck is with a doe all of the time during the rut. Find one on the prowl, and he'll trip over himself finding a tending grunt or clashing antlers.

•Don't give up. I remember the first year Minnesota moved to a week-long bucks-only season in the southeast. The rest of the gang went home on Monday night, but Larry Boughten and I hunted all week. It was late Thursday afternoon, and I was sitting in my stand, thinking we'd made a bad decision, when I heard the unmistakable sound of deer approaching hard. A long-necked doe busted over the ridge with a gnarly, 11-point buck hard on her heels. That buck was so charged up he was grunting non-stop. The buck was running so hard in his attempt to stay with the doe that when my slug broke his neck, he flipped end-over-end three times before dropping in a bed of leaves.

There are few places in the nation where the rut and the firearms deer season overlap. If you encounter such a situation, put that huge advantage to work for you this season.

Last gasp bowhunts

If you've still got an archery tag tucked away in your pocket late in the season, don't figure the gig is up. I'll not deceive you: There is nothing easy or particularly pleasant about last gasp bowhunting, but neither is it too late to affix that tag to the hind leg of a deer instead of relegating it to the unfilled tag file. Archery season closes one-half hour after sunset on New Year's Eve, and here is my game plan for the last couple of weeks of the season each year.

During a cold December, finding the animal's key food source is my No. 1 mission.

With snow on the ground, this is usually not a major undertaking. If a number of deer are really hammering a food source, one night's worth of tracks after a fresh snow will tell the story. In most cases, however, it takes two or three nights for deer to leave enough sign behind so that you can be sure you're hunting the prime food source and the main trail leading to that food source. This is high-speed scouting, because the sign, in the form of tracks and trails should be obvious.

I just hike the edges of the places deer will be

Any deer taken during the cold, often snowy hunting conditions of a Midwestern winter qualifies as a trophy.

feeding. In my part of the country this means harvested corn-fields, harvested soybean fields, and alfalfa stubble, usually in that order.

Deer prefer standing corn, but it's so rare in late December that only a few of you will be fortunate enough to have standing corn on the property you hunt. The next best situation is a field that has been picked but not chopped or tilled. If the wind blows off the snow so deer can get at the corn, they will feed in chopped fields. As a last resort, they'll even search a chisel-plowed field for the leftover kernels of grain.

Harvested but untilled soybean fields are attractive to deer in late December as well, especially if the combine left behind a good scattering of beans. There have been two times when I've seen deer ignore corn in favor of a harvested soybean field. In both cases I inspected the soybean field closely and found that waste soybeans were unusually abundant on those two fields, probably due to some malfunction with the combine.

Under very cold conditions, alfalfa becomes very brittle, loses many of its leaves to the winter wind, and is not very attractive to whitetail deer. Alfalfa draws deer in droves late in the season when an early, heavy snow covers the alfalfa field and insulates the plants. Under these conditions I have watched deer paw down through a foot or more of snow to reach the alfalfa, much of which remains green.

So-called truck gardens often are overlooked. I once watched a herd of a dozen does and fawns file into a pumpkin patch on a bitterly cold late season evening. The old does in the group would use quick jabs of their front hooves to split open the frozen pumpkins. It sounded like a bowling ball picking off the 10-pin for a spare. The fawns learn from the does. I've seen them do the same thing with squash and melons. Whatever vegetables remain attract deer when times get tough. Ditto for apple trees.

Though we don't have many locust trees in the Upper Midwest, I should mention that deer are very fond of the long, brown pods that fall from these trees. On a quiet evening, you can hear them crunching the frozen pods 100 yards away.

The nice thing about finding a woodlot or ridge where the deer have been scarfing up acorns is that usually the deer will begin feeding in these places by mid-afternoon because they feel more secure in the timber than in the open fields. The biggest buck I've ever seen on public land was munching acorns on New Year's

Eve on an oak-studded ridge in Minnesota's Whitewater Wildlife Management Area.

Even if there is a good supply of agricultural waste in your area, deer will spend some time each day browsing. If grain is in short supply, browse will dominate their diet. The best browse is from the tender tips of new growth. Those recently logged places are prime candidates for tender browse. Edges always provide deer with better browsing than the interior of big chunks of timber. This is because the edges get more sun during the growing season.

In hill country, when the weather turns cold, deer spend a lot of time on south-facing slopes. Not only is it warmer and out of the wind, but the browse is better on the south side of a hill than on the north.

Cover your hunting area fast. If you don't find plenty of tracks and a well-traveled trail or two leading to a food source, go somewhere else. The deer have.

BIOLOGY and HABITS

Where to find whitetails and when

L et's explore how the light, food, and weather dictate whitetail movement. The more you know about whitetail movement, the better the odds you'll be perched in a stand at the right place at the right time.

The food component

In farm country, deer have it made when it comes to chow. All through the summer months and into early fall when the crops are harvested, deer spend most of their time feeding in corn, soybean, and alfalfa fields. Sometimes these deer not only feed in the fields, they live there. In one study, a radio-collared buck spent an entire month in the fields. In another study, a mature buck wearing a homing device was tracked for an entire 24-hour period during late summer. The buck spent 22 of the 24 hours in the corn. Why not? The corn provided the buck with unlimited chow and the dense cover where it felt secure.

The study didn't indicate whether the two hours the buck spent out of the corn was during the day or at night, but I would bet it was at night, probably while the buck dined on adjacent soybeans or alfalfa. This is not an unusual situation to encounter during the first few weeks of the bow season.

Once the crops are harvested, it's a different story. Deer still feed on leftover corn and soybeans, but they also spend time browsing, feeding on grasses and weeds, and pigging out on acorns when they're available. In the hunting season, deer frequently sample all of these during a night of feeding, but it's rare that deer will not key on one particular food source. Finding that food source and then setting up your stand to take advantage of deer movement to that food source is the key to pre-rut success.

The light factor

White-tailed deer and every angler's favorite fish, the walleye, share a common trait in that they are crepuscular creatures, which simply means that they are most active during periods of low light, specifically dusk and dawn. This is the time when deer are most likely to move between bedding and feeding areas, which makes this prime time to intercept them. Deer move out of their beds and head toward feeding areas earlier on cloudy days than on clear days, which can give you a precious few minutes more on your evening stand. I've never noticed that cloud cover influences morning movement.

Influences of weather

Of all of the vagaries of weather, when it comes to whitetail movement, temperature is the first factor to consider. The balmy Novembers and Decembers of recent autumns in the Upper Midwest have reminded us that warm weather results in reduced deer movement. Decked out in their thick winter coats, deer find such weather uncomfortable, so they spend the daylight hours lying around in the shade and rarely budging from their day beds until the sun has set, sometimes later. That made for a lot of "no-show" stints on stand. Not much you can do during those conditions except hope that the last half hour of the evening and first hour of shooting light in the morning might produce a sighting or two.

When the weather cools after a warm period though, deer will be very active during a strong cold front.

Deer know when a storm is coming. I watch The Weather Channel a lot during deer season. If a storm is forecast to hit that night, I want to be on stand that afternoon. I've seen dozens of deer up and feeding at midday when a strong storm is brewing to the west. Deer instinctively know to fill their tanks before a storm so that they can go a day or two without feeding if the weather really is bad.

Deer don't mind feeding in a light snow or light rain. In fact I try to hunt when either condition prevails. But blizzards and thunderstorms are another story. I've spent more time than a grown man should hunting in both conditions and in every case, the deer were smarter than me and stayed put until the storm blew through. In my defense, however, I will admit that hunting during a heavy rain or snow has put me in position when the storm abates — prime time to hunt.

Whitetails don't move well in strong winds. A whitetail depends upon its acute sense of hearing, uncanny sense of smell, and motion-sensitive eyesight to detect danger. Wind interferes with all three senses, so the deer are reluctant to move at all and are usually super-skittish when they move. One study found that deer movement decreased when wind velocity reached 15 miles per hour. That number is pretty close to my own observations here at home, but in other parts of the country I've hunted where strong winds are more common, such as south Texas, Kansas, Nebraska, and eastern Colorado, a 15-mph wind is a gentle breeze, and it doesn't affect deer movement until it reaches gale proportions.

White-tailed deer are well adapted to handle the cold, but cold and wind is a bad combination. If it gets down into the single digits and a stiff wind is blowing, look for deer to move and feed in protected areas only.

Whitetails
in winter

While on a late-season muzzleloader deer hunt in southern Iowa during the first 10 days of 2001, I was reminded once again of how we humans tend to judge all of God's creatures and their actions against our own behavior.

It was below zero the first few days of the hunt, and with a foot of snow on the ground since early December, the conversation among the hunters on that trip centered on the tough winter the deer were facing. Some were concerned about deer starving to death. In fact, one friend purchased a whole wagonload of corn to help see the deer on his farm through the winter.

Those are noble thoughts and actions, but the truth of the matter is that even without the handouts, few deer die from starvation in Iowa. Deer in farm country get along just fine on a combination of left-over corn and natural browse. This diet provides deer with enough energy to withstand weeks of cold, even when less-than-ideal winter cover is available.

A whitetail's winter coat is comprised of a dense underfur and an "overcoat" of longer, hollow hair. This combination retains body heat so well that snow does not melt when it falls on them. Many times I've slipped up on deer nearly covered with snow as they lay in their winter beds. Once, during a late muzzleloader hunt after a severe blizzard, I crawled up within a few feet of a doe and fawn bedded down in 18 inches of new snow. The fawn must not have moved its head all night, because the snow was stacked up like a little dunce cap a good six inches high between its ears.

The white-tailed deer is well adapted to winter weather. What we humans consider "brutal" conditions comprise just another day in the woods to the stoic whitetail.

Now, go farther north and winter mortality becomes a legitimate concern. It's not a question of *if* deer are going to die during a typical winter in the forest country, it's just a matter of how many. That number depends upon a number of factors, the most important being average temperature, depth of the snow, herd density, and how long the severe weather persists. The availability of good browse and coniferous cover to decrease the effects of wind and bitter cold also is crucial.

Deer in the north country tend to "yard up" when winter descends. Deer vacate their summer ranges and migrate, sometimes covering 50 miles, although most travel under 10 miles, to reach the places where they traditionally have wintered. Fawns learn how to make the trip from their mothers and then pass it down to the next generation. Those who study such things suspect that this yarding behavior allows whitetails to conserve precious energy and serves as a defense against wolves, coyotes, and roaming packs of dogs. Over many generations, those deer that "yarded up" during the winter survived and lived to pass down this trait to their offspring, while those who tried to tough it out on their own, in unacceptable cover, perished.

I find it interesting that when winter sets in early, many deer will travel to the wintering areas, then disperse back to their summer ranges if the weather warms up again before the real onset of winter. When bad weather returns, the deer migrate back to their wintering area.

Deer often use the same trails to travel between their summer ranges and wintering areas, year after year. I have friends who hunt in Michigan's Upper Peninsula and in extreme northern Minnesota during the muzzleloader seasons who post on these trails in the hopes of intercepting deer marching toward the wintering areas. During years like 2000-01, which found deer on the move toward win-

The species we know as the white-tailed deer has survived thousands of north country winters and continues to thrive.

tering areas early in December, these patient hunters take some mighty impressive bucks.

If the white-tailed deer needed to consume as much food during the winter months as it consumes on a daily basis during the rest of the year, most deer would starve during a tough winter. But when winter grabs hold, white-tailed deer eat less — trimming their food intake by nearly a third. Obviously, this is not merely a matter of choice on the part of the deer, but a physiological adjustment, because even when deer have all of the food they want at their disposal, they still reduce the amount they consume by about one-third.

Deer also greatly reduce the amount they move during the winter. Most of their time during the winter months is spent bedded down in the best cover available. Deer seek bedding spots with good overhead cover (nothing beats conifers), which helps to reduce what is known as radiant heat loss and also to provide protection from heat-draining winds. When the weather is warm and sunny, deer congregate on south-facing slopes to take advantage of the warmth of the sun. In the coulee country of southeast Minnesota and western Wisconsin, it's not unusual to see a dozen or more deer on a south-facing slope on sunny, winter days.

I'm not trying to minimize the rigors of winter on the white-tailed deer. But except in the extreme northern part of the Midwest, winter mortality, even during a relatively harsh winter, is minimal. In the agricultural regions of the Midwest, far more deer will die on the highways than will starve in the woods.

Fawns: a rite of spring

Sometime right around my birthday (June 17, in case you were thinking of sending a lavish gift), our youngest daughter, Miss Kate, and I often cruise the backroads near our home in Byron during the last blush of day. Katie, who has developed a good eye for game, will holler, "There's a fawn, stop the truck!"

Evening drives to look for fawns are a rite of spring.

Actually, most fawns here in the Upper Midwest are born before my birthday, usually in late May and early June. The bulk of the fawns will drop during a two-week period. The reason most fawns are born at about the same time, instead of staggered out over a longer period, is that there are fewer losses to predation when there is an abundance of prey available for a short time. With the woods and fields full of newborn fawns, predators can find and kill a relatively small percentage of them. If births were spread out over a longer period, predators could account for a much higher percentage of the fawn crop losses.

You rarely see fawns during

An ability to remain perfectly still helps the young white-tailed deer survive and avoid predators. Photo by Ralph LaPlant

39

the first two weeks of their lives. This is because newborn fawns spend nearly all day and night curled in a tiny ball, usually in low vegetation, hiding from predators. After delivering her fawn, the doe sets about licking the fawn clean and eating all of the afterbirth. This helps ensure that predators will not be attracted to the area. The fawn then nurses, and the doe leads the fawn a short distance to the area where it wants the fawn to hide. The fawn lies down and stays put until the doe returns. If the doe has twins, or even triplets, it will not allow the siblings to lie down near each other. This helps ensure that even if a predator finds and kills one of the fawns, it likely will not discover the other fawn.

Young does allow twin fawns to bed closer to one another than mature does. This is one reason why fawn mortality is much higher for fawns born to first- and second-time mothers than for older does. Young does also are much more likely to abandon fawns than are older does, especially if the winter has been long and hard and the does are in poor condition.

The doe will visit the fawn only two or three times each day to allow the fawn to nurse and to lick the fawn clean. After each nursing session, the doe will lead the fawn a few hundred feet to a new place, where the fawn will again instinctively lie down to await the return of the doe. The fawn depends upon its excellent camouflage and ability to lie still-as-stone to avoid detection by predators.

You've often heard that a fawn is odor free, but this is not quite true. The doe does a good job of cleaning her fawn to keep it as clean as possible, but there is some odor. If there was not, predators such as coyotes would be much less successful at locating fawns during this stage. My hunting dogs have located, but not harmed, several newborn fawns over the years, and if they can smell them, a coyote or wolf certainly can.

One early June day, I was walking along the edge of a woods when my old Lab, Jack Daniels, began sniffing around in a patch of wild rhubarb. Because Jack had a thing for skunks, I figured he'd found another one of the smelly critters, and I raced to grab his collar and drag him away. Just as I reached for the dog, my leg pushed one of the big rhubarb leaves to the side and there under the leaf, curled in a tight ball and perfectly motionless was a tiny fawn. Its eyes were closed and I had to watch to determine whether the little tyke was breathing. Confirming this, I dragged Jack away, and we hurried from the area. Most fawns that people assume have been abandoned are not. Leave the fawn where you find it and odds are excellent that its mother will return.

After a couple of weeks, fawns gradually begin to spend more time with the doe. The fawns are now strong enough to escape predators. During the first two weeks, the fawns have doubled their weight. Also during this time, the doe will allow sibling fawns to bed closer to one another. With each passing day, the fawns spend more and more time in the company of the doe. This is when Miss Kate and I begin looking for them.

Most commonly we see them along the edge of a slough or woodlot, often nursing, sometimes eating a little new-growth alfalfa, other times running with carefree abandon with a sibling.

Fawns at this stage of their development totally are dependent upon the doe. Although they will eat small amounts of vegetation, their four-part stomach can't digest enough vegetation for them to survive. Studies have shown that this stage of development occurs at about eight weeks of age. After this age, fawns can survive without the doe's milk, although it's doubtful fawns deprived of milk at this age will develop as quickly as fawns that continue to nurse.

Because fawns spend all their time with the doe, they adopt her schedule, which means fawns learn to feed at dusk, dawn, a couple of times during the night, and a snack at mid-day. They will maintain this schedule their entire lives.

When a fawn is a couple of months old, the doe will begin to allow other deer to associate with it. Up until this time the doe will keep her fawn isolated from other deer. Usually the first deer that a fawn will encounter other than its mother and siblings will be other does, quite often does that did not give birth or lost their fawns. In almost all cases these deer will be related. This is the beginning of the fawn's introduction into the doe family-unit. Female fawns may be members of this family unit all of their lives. Male fawns will be driven off before they become sexually mature.

For many hunters, the only time they're interested in white-tailed deer is during the hunting season, but for me, it's a 365-day-per-year love affair. Watching a week-old fawn stand on unsure legs to suckle milk from a protective doe is as thrilling to me as watching an 8-point buck pick his way cautiously along a ridge in November.

If you happen to see a pickup pulled over this June with an old guy and a pretty, young girl eating a Dairy Queen treat and watching twin fawns chase each other around in circles, stop and wish me a happy birthday!

Find those appetizers

I've said it before: Late summer scouting to determine which field or fields deer use is as close to a sure-bet as you can get for success for the mid-September annual archery opener. But there's a big "unless" that usually follows that bit of gospel. That "unless" is the acorn drop.

If acorns start dropping between the time you pinpoint those entry points to the fields and opening day, they can quickly snuff out that sure-fire bet.

It's not that deer suddenly abandon the alfalfa or soybeans. They're still munching on the tasty legumes; it's just that the deer get delayed on their trip to the field. Instead of stepping into the field a half hour or even a full hour before the end of shooting hours, as has been their habit all summer, they now

Call them "appletizers." Though the acorns of white oaks often sidetrack field-bound, early season whitetails, apple trees may be the culprit, too.

hang back in the woods munching acorns for an hour or so after getting out of their beds. They don't make it to the fields until after dark.

It's like going out to a favorite steakhouse. When I walk in, I've got my heart set on a big rib-eye served medium rare. But when our waitress takes our order she notes the special on buffalo wings. So we order the appetizer. We will still eat that rib-eye, but we've delayed the main course.

The mid-September opening of the archery season often coincides with the first real windfall of acorns. I can't begin to remember all of the times I've climbed into my stand brimming with confidence on the first evening of the season only to climb down a couple of hours later shaking my head and wondering what happened to my best-laid plan. The culprit is the fruit of the oak tree, and when this happens, you must find the oaks providing the appetizers, then set up your stand. This usually is not difficult.

Start at the field and backtrack the entry trail as far as you can. Look for oaks. Deer will eat acorns from any oak tree, but they prefer those of the white oak. In Minnesota we have red oaks and white oaks. The easiest way to differentiate between the two in summer or fall is to look at the leaves. Red oaks have leaves with pointed ends, while the lobes of the white oak leaves are rounded.

When you find a white oak, look around for acorns on the ground, droppings, and if the ground is soft, deer tracks. If the drop is heavy enough to be short-stopping your deer, you'll feel acorns under your feet. Sometimes there will be a few buck rubs in the vicinity, but if not, do not assume that a buck is not feeding under the tree or trees you locate. Take the prevailing wind into account and hang a stand.

Although it's always disappointing when deer do not show up at a field as planned, if they are being short-stopped by acorns somewhere en route, I look upon it as a positive instead of a negative. Now I have a good early season morning stand as well as a fine evening stand.

Field edges make lousy morning stands because the deer are often in the field when you arrive, you spook them, and that's that. But if you can slip into your stand in the oaks before first light without letting deer in the field see or smell you, you have a very good chance of seeing some morning action as the deer filter through and scarf up a few acorns as they return to their daytime bedding cover.

Although the short-stopping culprit usually is acorns, on several occasions I've found apples to be the appetizer keeping the deer from getting right to the main course. Deer have a sweet tooth, and when the apples are falling, deer are attracted to them.

So if the deer don't show up in the field you've scouted, don't just assume that you, or someone else, have spooked them. Instead, find those appetizers.

Whitetails
out of the gate

A number of years ago when the bowhunting world was just starting to take notice of Myles Keller — an archer from southern Minnesota with an unmatched knack for taking Pope and Young bucks — I spent a couple of hours interviewing Keller for a bowhunting article.

One thing that surprised me in that interview was the number of big bucks Myles has taken, not during the rut (far and away the most heralded portion of the hunting season, especially when talking mature bucks) but rather during the early part of the season.

Although my record on big bucks does not approach that of Myles Keller, I share his fondness for whitetails out of the gate. No matter if you're hunting for "a deer" or the buck of a lifetime, those first few days and weeks of the season can provide you with some of the best action of the entire season. Here is why.

Predictability

When the archery deer season opens in mid-September, whitetails usually are still in their late summer pattern. Through the heat of July and August and right into September, deer live the easy life. Food is abundant and nutritious, and with nobody bothering them, deer spend the late summer weeks chowing down and lying around in the shade chewing their cud. If ever a white-tailed deer relaxes, it's during this time period.

At no other time of the season will deer be as predictable in their habits. Even mature bucks show up evening after evening to feed in crop fields. Although deer consume grass, forbs, and the first mast of acorns at this time of the year, farm crops make up the bulk of their late-summer diet, where available. Tops on the list is soybeans. As long as the soybean plant continues to grow, deer will roam through the belly-high rows nipping off tender new growth from the tops of the plants.

Soybeans remain number one until the plant is done growing, either as a result of the plant reaching maturity, or more often, the result of a killing frost. Then they'll turn their attention to alfalfa. Some years, the middle of September finds the soybean plants still growing and deer keying on them, but other years, it's alfalfa.

I locate deer feeding in a soybean field while scouting in August and early September, then search for the nearest alfalfa field. If the soybeans cease growing or are harvested before the season opens, I want to know where the nearest alfalfa field exists, because nine times out of 10, the same deer using the soybean field will visit the alfalfa field.

Inside the ropes

Once you locate the deer and secure permission to hunt, determine where to hang your stands. Usually I spend an evening or two watching the field (from a safe distance to avoid spooking the deer) to see where they're entering the field. Often deer will enter a field using an obvious route such as a fenceline, a finger of timber jutting into the field, or maybe a field road.

Once I've determined where deer are most likely to enter a field, I hang a stand to cover the entrance trail and the edge of the field. If deer are entering the field at random points, I'll hang a stand or put up a ground blind along the edge of the field and rely upon a buck decoy to draw the buck to me. Even though bucks are not

Seasoned bowhunters know you can't beat the combination of predictable, unpressured deer, ample food, and mild weather of the early season.

aggressive at this time of the year, a buck decoy will get the attention of another buck. Often the buck will investigate the decoy out of curiosity. My friend Dennis Williams of Eyota, Minn., killed a beautiful 150-inch, 10-point with that very tactic.

As soon as a buck has any inkling of hunting presence, you can forget about him wandering into the field while shooting light remains. However, this does not mean you should give up on him. Rarely will a buck abandon a prime food source because of a little human interference. Instead, he'll hold back in cover and browse until it's dark. A stand 30 to 60 yards back in the cover from which the buck exited is the best way to take advantage of this trait.

Speaking of pressure

If you're fortunate enough to have exclusive hunting rights to a piece of secluded property, you might milk a couple of weeks out of the early season, but those are rare cases. For those of us who hunt on public land or share private property with other hunters, a few days, or maybe a week is all you'll get. By then small game hunters, upland bird hunters, or other bowhunters have tipped off the deer.

Squeeze as many days as you can out of the early season period. Take precautions to ensure that you disturb the deer as little as possible. Here are some ways to minimize your impact.

• The easiest way to ruin a stand and quite possibly the whole field, is to let deer see you climb down from your stand at the end of an evening. But what about when there are deer below your stand at the end of shooting hours?

The slickest trick is to have someone drive up to the field (be sure you have permission) to pick you up. When the vehicle arrives on the scene, the deer will scamper off into the woods, giving you enough time to climb down and hustle to the vehicle. If possible, have the vehicle drive right up to the base of the tree. Because deer are accustomed to vehicles, the deer will return to the field to feed when it departs.

If you cannot arrange to have someone pick you up, you have two other options. One, wait until it's dark, climb down slowly and carefully and then slip out the back way without showing yourself to the deer in the field. Do this cautiously, and you will see how tolerant deer are of the little noises you make. They probably think it's just raccoons or other critters.

Another option that has been successful for me is to use my voice to bark like a dog — a big dog, hungry for venison. The deer will run from the field, which gives me time to climb down and exit.

• Don't hunt the field in the mornings. You'll scare off any deer in the field. If you want to hunt mornings, do so well away from the field you plan to hunt in the evening, and make sure that you can access the morning stand without disturbing deer in the field.

• The best morning stands I've found are along fencelines and creek bottoms. In farm country, these two features comprise the whitetail's equivalent of our highway system.

• If you have a number of equally good fields, rotate your hunting efforts to spread out the pressure, but if you only have one field, hunt it every evening that the wind is right. The early season is a short window of opportunity, and you don't want to miss out in fear of over-hunting the spot.

I've had many bowhunters tell me that they don't even bother to start hunting until late October when the bucks crank up for the rut. One look at that wall full of trophies Myles Keller has collected over the years should convince anyone that whitetails right out of the gate are worth the effort.

The acorn factor

Deer are so visible around field edges early in the season that sometimes one of the most dependable early season food sources gets overlooked. I'm talking acorns, of course. Although deer will eat just about anything that grows, just like us they have their favorite foods, and acorns, especially from white oaks, are near the top of the list.

October is often thought of as the month to be hunting stands of white oak, though during a good mast year, plenty of acorns are falling in September (I've seen them fall in August) to keep deer interested. Locate some good mast trees and you have the location for excellent early season action. I carry good binoculars with me and scan the upper branches of white oaks looking for acorns. Once you get used to looking for them, it's easy to spot trees carrying the heaviest crop of nuts. These are the trees you want to hunt near. I know hunters who own land and routinely fertilize a few oak trees on their property so that these trees will produce bumper crops of acorns.

In the evening, deer often will spend some time scarfing acorns before browsing the soybean or alfalfa fields. Think of it as whitetail hors d'oeuvres. This might not mean much to you as long as the deer are still arriving at the field during shooting hours, but deer react quickly to hunting pressure. After a week or two most of the deer will not enter the field until after dark. That doesn't mean the deer are staying in bed until then. Odds are good they're feeding on acorns while they wait for darkness.

I've seen deer crunching acorns a good two hours before the end of shooting hours, especially the youngsters, which like youngsters of every species are always hungry. I always get a kick out of watching a fawn trying to crack a big, old acorn. They roll the things around in their mouth like a jaw-breaker. On a calm, quiet evening you can hear them trying to get at the meat of the acorn. Those little quirks of nature are what makes bowhunting so enjoyable.

If you like big bucks, I don't know of a better evening location than a mast-bearing stand of white oaks between the buck's bedding area and the fields where he feeds at night.

After the first couple days of the season, the big boys probably won't step into the open until last light, but they will rise from their beds, browse a bit, and scarf up a few acorns on their way to the main course. Intercept them here.

Field edges make lousy morning stand sites, but a stand of acorn-bearing oaks is ideal. Just as deer will feed on the acorns before they hit the fields in the evening, the same deer often will take time on the trip back to bed at dawn to munch on the tasty nuts. Find a stand of oaks that you can access without having to cross the fields and you have a great early season morning stand.

Whenever I hunt over acorns, I always carry a few small rocks in my pocket. When acorns are thick on the ground, deer have little trouble finding them, but it's rarely that easy. Deer quickly learn to listen for the sound of an acorn hitting the carpet of leaves below. When they hear the "plop" of an acorn, they wander over to

The acorn search accelerates as deer begin spending more shooting time in the woods and less time in the fields.

51

find it. I've seen young deer race each other to the site of a falling acorn. A stone sounds just like an acorn when it falls to the leaves. Pretty sneaky.

Go ahead and concentrate on the fields until that action fizzles. But when it does, (and it will) don't hang up your bow. Instead, look for acorns. The deer already have found them.

The rut stuff

When it comes to the whitetail rut, there are a lot of myths, misconceptions, and poor information being passed from hunter to hunter and generation to generation. Here is some "rut stuff," which is also the "right stuff."

• Back when Minnesota held its first special muzzleloader season, one of my partners returned to camp the first evening and reported that "the rut must have been a real bust this year." I asked him why.

"I saw three does today and all of them had a fawn with them," he said matter-of-factly. "When a doe breeds, she kicks her fawns away so that they can't see what is happening."

I laughed so loud that the old, half-deaf farm dog on Earl Timm's place, behind which we were camping, heard me howling and joined right in.

Actually, my hunting partner was partially correct. Prior to breeding, a doe will chase away her fawns. But once the estrous cycle has passed, the doe

Community scrapes are a great place to hunt if you want action but don't care about size. Just remember, mature bucks usually don't share scrapes.

53

will allow the doe-fawn to rejoin her. A buck fawn, however, must strike off on his own to adopt a new home range. That's how nature prevents inbreeding.

•Huge scrapes nearly always are "community scrapes," which means that three, four, or as many as a half dozen different bucks visit the scrape. Each buck enlarges the scrape a little when it visits, and that's how the scrapes grow.

Community scrapes are great places to hunt if you want action and don't care about size. But if you have your sights on a mature buck, a community scrape is a poor bet for locating the dominant buck. Most times, gangs of young bucks develop a community scrape. Mature bucks usually don't share their scrapes.

•Speaking of community scrapes, one year a friend of mine set up a remote control camera on a big community scrape. The next day, all 24 exposures were gone. My friend went over the 24 pictures with a magnifying glass to identify the bucks that had visited the scrape. Guess how many bucks had paid a visit in one night?

Would you believe 19! As a footnote, I'd add that I hunted near that community scrape for the next two days and saw just one buck. Go figure.

•A big difference between young bucks and mature bucks: While young bucks usually approach a scrape to check it for scent, a mature buck often will scent-check the scrape from downwind. This is especially common when the scrape is in the open, such as on the edge of a field. Remember this when you position your stand.

•When a doe visits a scrape she is able to sniff the combination of urine and tarsal gland scent left behind by the buck that made the scrape and determine, through smell alone, whether or not the buck is a suitable mate. Seems a lot simpler than the human process.

•An active scrape will always have an overhanging branch on which the buck rubs his face and antlers, depositing scent from his forehead gland and pre-orbital glands, which are located in the corner of each eye, in the process. The buck also will chew and lick the branch, which adds saliva to the branch. And because bucks frequently lick their tarsal glands during the rut, they also add tarsal gland scent and urine to the overhanging branch. All of this scent is a buck's way of announcing that he's claiming the area as his breeding grounds.

• If you have the time, hunt all day when bucks are scraping. I've seen bucks visit scrapes during the midday hours when most hunters are back at camp. New research has confirmed my own experiences. The peak time for a buck to revisit an existing scrape during shooting hours was 2 p.m.

• Many old-timers believe the first good cold snap in November triggers the rut, but the truth is that the shorter days of fall send a signal to the deer's brain to fire up the old hormones. There is, however, certainly a connection between the weather and daytime rut activity. In warm weather, deer chase and breed at night, when it's more comfortable for them.

• Little scrapes are made by little bucks. A mature buck will make a scrape that's at least 18 inches in diameter, but usually larger, sometimes five or six times that large.

• While I'm on the subject of scrapes, some very interesting research has shown that bucks lay out their scrape lines in distinct north-south lines as well as east-west lines. Find where these cross — I can't think of a better place for a stand.

The October 'mini-rut'

For years, I kept this information to myself, not because I was being selfish, but because I thought people would think me crazy to bring it up.

You see, for the past 15 years, I've noticed that sometime between Oct. 11 and Oct. 15, a spurt of buck activity occurs that has all of the classic features of the rut. I've seen an increase in scraping activity, rubs, fighting, chasing, and even bucks trailing and tending does during this short period.

But I kept my mouth shut. Then a couple of years ago, I sat down to supper on the evening of Oct. 13 with my friend Tom Indrebo, who with his wife, Laurie, runs Bluff Country Outfitters in Wisconsin's justifiably famed Buffalo County. Tom is more than an excellent outfitter; he's a serious student of whitetail behavior and knows as much about the white-tailed deer as anyone I've ever met. So I took a chance and shared with Tom what I'd seen that day in October.

What I had seen was seven different bucks, all of them engaged in some rut-related activity. The center of all the attention was a single doe. She was an old doe, easily evidenced by the hump nose, sagging back, drooping belly and stiff gait. The biggest of the seven bucks, a dandy 9-pointer that I would have shot had he given me the opportunity, finally herded the old gal off the oak flat I was hunting.

Tom listened to my description of the activities of that day and to my accounts of similar experiences on those dates over the years. He didn't interrupt, but I could tell by his eyes that he recognized the situation. When I took a breather and reached for a couple more cookies and the coffee pot, Tom, in his slow, methodical manner, told me I was not crazy, but that he too had observed the same type of rut behavior during the same dates for many years. That made me feel better. At least if I was crazy, I now had company!

You won't find anything in the books on this October mini-rut, and I have not found a whitetail biologist who puts much stock in such a theory, but then I don't put much stock in books and charts and never-ending studies either. I believe what I see.

My guess is that in every deer herd there is probably a doe or two that enters estrus a few weeks before the others. Friends who raise deer tell me this is not uncommon in captive herds. From my experience, the doe is an old one, but I have no way of knowing if this always is the case.

Many bowhunters consider mid-October to be a time of inactivity in the deer woods. Often, you hear of this period referred to as the "October lull." But I look forward to that short span between Oct. 11 and 15. I use the same tactics then that I will use during the November rut. I grunt, doe bleat, and rattle frequently during this time period.

Most of the time I hunt over a decoy during these dates, although if I'm hunting thick cover, I don't use a decoy. I hunt over a lot of mock scrapes and use a lot of deer scents for doctoring existing scrapes, laying down scent trails, and applying scent wicks around my stand.

This October action often is isolated, so I spend a lot of time looking for sign that can tip me off to where to hunt. Find an area torn up with fresh scrapes or just the haphazard maze of overturned leaves where deer have been chasing. Often I spend time in "observation stands." These stands allow me to monitor a

The mid-October mini-rut exists! Be prepared by monitoring signs of rutting, like rubs, and keep your grunt tube and rattling antlers handy.

good chunk of country. On a quiet morning or evening, you can, if you listen closely, hear a buck grunt or a doe bleat from a surprisingly long distance. You can hear deer chasing each other through dry, or frost-coated leaves from an even greater distance.

Two Octobers ago, on one of those chilly, calm mornings when I could hear the farmer's dog yapping a mile down the valley, I was perched in one of my observation stands looking and listening when I heard the unmistakable sound of running deer. The leaves were dry, and the deer made a lot of racket. I was having a hard time getting a fix on the exact location of the sound. Then I heard the deer splash through water.

The only water was the little creek down in the pasture, so I climbed down and headed in that direction. The racket subsided before I arrived, but as I slipped across the creek and into the timber on the other side, I could tell from overturned leaves that a lot of chasing had been taking place.

A string of five scrapes pock-marked the ridge just above the creek. All had been worked recently. I hung my stand within range of the largest of the scrapes, put a silhouette decoy 20 yards upwind, hung a half dozen scent wicks doctored with doe-in-estrus urine around my stand, climbed up and settled in for the day.

It was 8:30 a.m. By dark I had seen five different bucks. The three smaller bucks had all come into the decoy and offered me plenty of opportunities for a shot, but I was holding out for a mature buck. The two larger bucks, one a 10-pointer with a broken brow tine and the other a heavy-antlered 8-point, were both in hot pursuit of an old doe.

Twice they trailed the old gal past my stand, but I couldn't get a shot either time, and they ignored my pleading grunts, bleats, and the decoy. No, I never dropped the string that Oct. 14, 1999, but I had the time of my life.

Isn't that what it's all about anyway?

Remember this four-letter word: F-O-O-D

If you're hunting deer in December, whether via bow and arrow or muzzleloader, food is the four-letter word you want to remember. All across the north country, the main emphasis for all deer at that time is making sure they get plenty of food. The big bucks, the ones that participated most actively in the rut, are especially hungry this time of year.

When a mature whitetail buck gets into the business of procreating the species, he takes his mission so seriously that he ignores eating. Some bucks will lose up to a quarter of their body weight during the rut. I've skinned out big bucks taken at the end of the rut that did not have a speck of body fat on their backstraps or rumps. That same buck taken in October or early November would have a half-inch-plus of white fat layered between hide and meat.

A buck instinctively knows that in order to survive the upcoming winter he had better put that fat back on after the rut or face the consequences. A buck that enters the winter lean will not survive if

In December, if you're not keyed in on the food source, you're in for a long, cold, boring wait. Clancy's advice: Find the food, then hunt.

59

the cold is long and the snow deep.

When a buck turns his attention from sex to food, that buck becomes easily patterned if you can locate his food source. That's the trick. I can't tell you what it will be, because it varies according to habitat. In the agricultural regions, you can't beat corn. Standing corn is best if you can find it. Next best is a field that has been picked but not chopped.

If that's not available, deer will flock to a field where the stalks have been chopped but the ground not worked. Once the field has been plowed, it lacks drawing power. Sure there are a few kernels of corn available mixed in with the dirt, but the pickings are too lean to consistently attract deer.

I've seen times when deer have flocked to harvested soybean fields and other times when they'll ignore similar fields. Walking through the fields, it was easy to see why. The fields deer are attracted to have plenty of soybeans scattered on the ground, and the fields they ignore are nearly devoid of waste grain. Alfalfa is not a big draw in December. Deer are into carbohydrates and fat now, not protein, which is what alfalfa is all about. However, in areas where alfalfa was the only readily available food source, I've seen many whitetails paw through a foot of snow to get at the buried greens.

Speaking of greens, if you find green vegetation in the woods you're hunting, examine it closely. You are likely to see where deer have been eating. In hilly country, look for green vegetation down in the bottom of steep draws and gullies. And don't forget acorns. When the ground is littered with acorns, all of the turkeys, squirrels, bears, deer, and other critters that relish the fallen fruit cannot get all of the acorns eaten in October and November so there are acorns left over for the late season. Once there is snow on the ground, it's easy to see if deer have been pawing through the snow looking for acorns. And don't dismiss an area just because it is pockmarked with the oval-shaped scratching that indicates that wild turkeys have been using their big feet to help them find acorns. Many times I've watched deer follow along right behind the turkeys, eating the acorns the turkeys uncover.

Maybe it's tender browse from an area that was burned over or logged off a year or two ago that attracts the deer. Or maybe a hidden meadow, cedar swamp, or those leftover pumpkins in your neighbor's garden. Don't laugh, deer will eat almost anything when winter is approaching.

One December I watched two roly-poly fawns all decked out in their furry winter coats try, without much success, to bite a chunk out of some frozen pumpkins. When the old doe walked out she strode up to a pumpkin, cocked a front leg, and brought it down on that pumpkin with enough force to split the pumpkin into a half dozen pieces. Sounded like a .410 going off on that cold winter evening. The fawns learned a lesson that day.

Late season
deer hunting

I probably spend as many days freezing my butt off in a tree-stand in December and the first part of January as any hunter. Part of the reason for this, as Nancy Clancy is quick to remind me, is that I have all of these tags left come December because I'm not smart enough (or good enough) to fill them when the weather is balmy in September, October, and November.

The girl has a point. But be that as it may, while I would never claim to possess expert status in any faction of whitetail hunting, I have considerable experience hunting late in the season via bow and arrow, and muzzleloader.

For many years I tried to plan my late-season, out-of-state hunts around the worst winter weather possible. I would stay glued to The Weather Channel and when a real doozy of a winter storm was predicted, I would throw my stuff in the pickup and head for Wisconsin, Michigan, Illinois, or maybe just out the back door to bowhunt in Minnesota. Yes, I took some good bucks by adhering to my "bad weather equals big bucks" theory, but today, I'm also convinced that I probably missed out on the best hunting of the late season by waiting for the worst of what winter could dish out.

There are two primary reasons for this. One, once the primary rut ends, the bucks, especially the biggest bucks, turn their attention to food. They have to if they are going to survive the winter. This singleness of purpose occurs regardless of the weather when the rut ends. Extreme cold and deep snow are not needed to force bucks to spend more time at the chow line than they normally would.

When their breeding duties end, bucks focus on laying on the fat, regardless of the weather. However, when we get cold and snow early in the late season, they throw deer into a panic. In a recent magazine article, I compared the first winter storm of the season to having your favorite supermarket burn down during the night. Deer must wonder where they'll find their next meal when their world is suddenly buried under a foot of wet, heavy snow. The best late-season hunting does not occur after winter weather has blasted us for weeks, but rather in the wake of that first winter wake-up call.

The other reason why I now believe this to be true is that although it would seem logical that deer would require more food as winter progresses, the opposite is true. As a means of surviving difficult winters, a whitetail's metabolic activity and thyroid functions actually decrease as the days grow shorter. This allows the whitetail to survive nicely with up to 30 percent less food than it normally consumes. When you combine this drop in food requirements with the fact that as a whitetail adjusts its body to the snow and cold, it conserves energy by reducing movement by up to 50 percent. That simply means they spend more time bedded and less time on their feet, so as the late season progresses, your odds of scoring do not improve, they get worse.

Here is another recent change in my late-season thinking. For many years I thought the very best chance to take a buck was when the weather was at its worst. Give me a raging blizzard, minus 20-degree temperatures and throw in a howling northwest wind and I was one happy (if frozen) late-season hunter. If the weather warmed up, say into the 20s or heaven-forbid, even the 30s, I slipped into a deep funk. I was sure that the warm weather meant that the deer would

Late-season success doesn't always require miserable weather. In fact, warm December days usually mean active, huntable deer.

remain bedded until after dark in the evening and that my odds of seeing them during shooting hours were nearly non-existent.

But I know now that the opposite is true. When the weather is at its worst, the deer bed down and don't move much. When it warms up, the deer once again become active, which means they head for the food source earlier in the day.

By the way, warm spells on the heels of a winter storm are also the best times to hunt mornings during the late season. When the weather is brutal, morning hunting is a waste of time, because deer remain bedded during the traditional early morning hours as these hours often are the coldest period of the day. But during a warm-up, deer often linger and browse for several hours in the morning before bedding down. This makes morning hunts in or near the bedding area very productive when the weather warms up.

If you're like me and usually have an unfilled tag in your pocket come late season, I hope this little discussion of December-January tactics will help make your last-ditch hunts more productive.

Forget the second rut

In early December, you can't pick up a deer hunting magazine without finding a story or two about how to hunt the so-called second rut. All of this attention has left many late-season hunters with the mistaken impression that rut activity should be hot and heavy during December. Nothing could be further from the truth.

Sure, some breeding takes place in December. A few of the adult does that either were not bred or did not conceive after being bred during their November estrus will cycle back in for another estrus sometime in December. In the central and southern portions of Minnesota, Wiscon-sin, and Michigan, there also will be some female fawns experiencing their first estrous cycle this month. Opinions vary on just how many of these young-of-the-year does actually will be bred, but many students of whitetails believe that at least one-quarter of them will be bred this month.

That sounds like a lot of breeding activity, but when compared to

Though you might stumble into a so-called second rut buck late in the season, make locating key food sources your first priority during December deer hunting.

65

the November rut, the "second rut" is a real dud. For the past 10 years, I've spent 20 or more days in December and early January hunting via bow or muzzleloader in Minnesota, Wisconsin, Iowa, Illinois, or northern Missouri, all places where the second rut occurs. During those 200-plus days I've seen significant second-rut activity only a dozen times.

My own experiences hunting during this period and those of others whose experiences have been similar to mine have convinced me that building a game plan for hunting the late season around the second rut is a waste of time and effort. Put that time and effort into locating the prime food source in the area you're hunting and you'll be ahead of the game.

By locating the prime food source and hunting either the food source itself or trails leading from it to the bedding areas, you are in prime position to take advantage of any secondary breeding activity. Why? Because December bucks are not actively seeking estrous does. In November, bucks constantly are looking for a receptive doe, but by this month, those bucks, although still willing to do the job if the opportunity presents itself, are more concerned with finding and consuming high-quality forage before the onset of winter.

Most of the December rut activity I've witnessed has occurred at the food source. Here's what usually happens: A few does and fawns make their way to a harvested cornfield. One of them is in heat. The first buck on the scene picks up the scent of the estrous doe and starts chasing her around the field. Other bucks, attracted by the scent of the estrous doe, or the chasing, join in the party.

It's unusual for a doe in heat in December to attract just a single buck. I've seen as many as seven bucks chasing a single estrous doe. Once, in Iowa, I watched five mature bucks, the largest a huge nontypical, hounding a doe-fawn in heat. When it happens, second-rut activity is certainly exciting, but you just can't count on it.

If you find fresh scrapes or rubs this month, don't get too excited. I've spent more days than I care to admit sitting over December scrapes and rubs waiting for the buck that made them. I could just as well have been ice fishing.

During an average December I'll bowhunt in Wisconsin, Minnesota, and Michigan and follow that up with a late-season muzzleloader hunt, say in southern Iowa or Illinois. I could encounter some secondary rut activity on any of those hunts, but I'm not betting on it. If I can locate the main food source (the chow being used by the bulk of the deer in the area, including the larger bucks), I bet that I'm going to see deer — second rut or no second rut. If I happen to get lucky and encounter some secondary rut activity, good for me, but I don't count on it. Unless you like being disappointed, you should not pin your late-season hopes on the second rut, either.

EQUIPMENT STRATEGIES

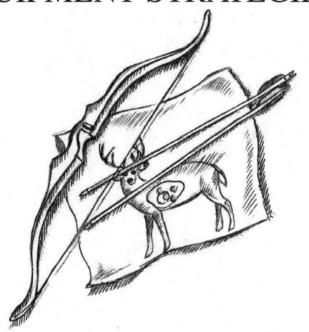

Optics for whitetail hunting

One of the great things about being an outdoors writer is that once you've built a reputation (you hope a good one) in the business, companies ask you to test their products in the field or on the range. These products usually must be returned to the manufacturer, but it gives a writer an opportunity to field test and compare products.

This arrangement has given me an opportunity to test optics manufactured by Nikon, Leica, Swarovski, Leupold, Simmons, Weaver, Bausch & Lomb, Bushnell, Redfield, Weaver, Pentax, Steiner, Brunton, Burris, and Tasco. Having had an opportunity to use a wide variety of sporting optics during the past decade, I've developed a few opinions on what works and what does not.

Rifle scopes

My first "real" scope was an old K-4 Weaver mounted atop a

Serious whitetail hunters should consider all forms of outdoor optics — including scopes, binoculars, and rangefinders — mandatory hunting equipment.

sporterized Springfield .30-06. I would not feel handicapped if forced to hunt with that old straight four-power scope for the rest of my days. In fact, I'm convinced that many deer hunters would be better off with a fixed four-power scope on their rifles than with the variable-power scopes 99 percent of today's hunters use. Why? Because many hunters cannot resist cranking that variable power scope up to its maximum magnification.

The reasoning seems to be that if 3X is good, then 9X must be three times better. The problem of too much magnification is even greater today as manufacturers respond to the "more must be better" cry and build variable power scopes with top-end magnifications suited to studying moon craters.

When you increase the magnification on a variable-power scope, you decrease the field-of-view. Trying to find a buck standing still in a tangle of popple is tough enough at 9X; getting on a moving buck is all but impossible. How many times have you heard, "I was walking back to camp when the biggest buck I've ever seen jumped up right in front of me, but when I tried to get on him, all I could see was hair. Before I could crank my scope down to low power, he was gone."

Don't get me wrong. I'm not condemning variable power scopes for deer hunting. On centerfire rifles I like something in the 2x7 to 3x9 range. On shotguns I like straight 2.5X, 3X or 4X or a low-power variable in the 1.5x5 to 2x7 range. Ditto for muzzle-loaders, although remember that in some states, including Minnesota, you cannot use a scope on a muzzleloader during the special blackpowder season. Even with these relatively low top-end magnification variables, I keep the magnification set at the lowest setting. Low magnification makes it easy to find the target and to stay with a moving deer. Only twice can I recall cranking the power up to make a longer shot.

Many scopes today feature 50mm and larger objective lenses. The sales pitch says the large objective lens will gather more light when light is poor. That's an honest sales pitch. The problem is that during the four decades I've spent hunting deer across North America, during every conceivable type of weather, I've yet to encounter light conditions so poor during legal shooting hours that a 40mm or even a 30mm objective lens does not gather sufficient light for an accurate shot.

Scopes with 50mm objective lenses are more expensive and weigh more than scopes of comparable quality featuring 40mm objectives. And on some rifles, that big objective lens dictates that the scope be mounted very high so that the objective lens can clear the barrel. This makes it difficult to get your cheek nestled on the comb of the stock where it belongs, and that factor will affect accuracy every time.

I've used the least expensive scopes on the market and those costing several times the value of many rifles. My tastes run somewhere in the middle. The least expensive scopes are more likely to develop problems such as broken crosshairs or faulty seals, which lead to fogging. The most expensive are, in my judgement, not worth the price. There are lots of good, high quality scopes in the $250 to $450 range that will serve you a lifetime.

Binoculars

I use binoculars a lot when hunting deer. Without them, you'll miss seeing a lot of deer. I'm constantly scanning the timber with binoculars when hunting. Countless times the binoculars have picked up the twitch of a tail, the wiggle of an ear, or just a patch of brown, gray, white, or black that looked out of place and proved to be part of a deer.

I've read that when it comes to optics, you get what you pay for, but I'm not convinced that necessarily is true. I've hunted with binoculars costing over a grand, and while they were bright, clear, and sharp, I can't say that my eyes could discern much difference between the most expensive binoculars and those costing a third as much. You can buy some mighty fine binoculars for $300.

If $300 is out of your price range, don't let that be an excuse for hunting without binoculars. I carried an ultra-cheap pair of compact binoculars that set me back the royal sum of $39.95 for many years. No, they were not bright, sharp, or clear, and if you stared through them for long, you ended up with Excedrin headache No. 101, but I saw a lot of deer with those cheap specs.

Speaking of compacts, I'm not a big fan. The ones I've used (several) have had poor light-gathering abilities, narrow field of view, and were almost impossible to use while wearing eyeglasses.

Full-size binoculars are great for use from the seat of the truck, but are too big and bulky for the woods. I stick with mid-size binoculars and prefer a 7x35 or 8x40 for whitetail duty.

EQUIPMENT STRATEGIES
I missed – a baker's dozen of excuses

It has been my great reward to have spent more hours in deer camps around the country than a man probably should, or that a more responsible person ever would. Be that as it may, I got to thinking when I was writing a Strictly Whitetails piece on practicing, about all of the excuses for missed opportunities I've heard over the years. I'll admit that I've uttered a few of them myself. Here are some of my favorites.

One: *"I missed."*

I like this one. No excuses. Straight and to the point. Rarely heard, however.

Two: *"I must have hit a twig."*

Just another way of saying, "I missed," but not as classy.

Three: *"I shot right over his back."*

Why is it that when 90 percent of the deer are killed at ranges of under 100 yards, nearly everyone wants to sight in their guns to impact an inch or two high at 100 yards instead of dead-on? Since even the flattest shooting of calibers have a rainbow trajectory, even over that first 100 yards, and since many hunters are in the habit (a bad one) of holding a little high anyway, guess where the projectile goes when a buck is standing broadside at 50 yards?

Four: *"I couldn't find him in the scope."*

You heard this excuse less frequently back in the days when most hunters had straight 4X scopes. But now, with most hunters using variable-power scopes (see previous chapter), some with enough magnification to study Pleiades, this excuse is heard with sickening regularity. Keep your scope set on the lowest magnification, and when that buck jumps up or suddenly appears at 30 yards, you won't have any trouble finding him.

Five: *"My scope was fogged up."*

Scopes don't fog up on their own, you have to breathe on them. Anti-fog spray helps.

Six: *"My safety was stuck."*

Translation: I didn't get the safety all of the way off. Strictly a matter of familiarity.

Seven: *"I missed with the first shot and then my @#@!@# gun jammed."*

Sometimes a gun will malfunction, but usually it is operator error. Short-stroking, which means not fully extending the bolt, lever or forearm, is a common culprit with pumps, lever-actions, and bolt-actions. With semi-autos, it's usually the result of a dirty action.

Eight:. *"I'm shooting a .396 Super-Sonic-Turbo-Blaster! That buck should have been flattened."*

Big time flinch! I've got nothing against the magnum calibers, but most deer hunters would shoot a low recoil caliber such as a .25-06, 7mm-08 or .270 better (and more often) than they do a bellowing, bucking magnum, and the deer would be just as dead. Anytime I see a hunter in deer camp with a caliber better suited to brown bears or Cape buffalo, I'm always suspect.

Nine: *"My stock got hung up in my coat and I couldn't get it to my shoulder."*

Do a little shooting with your hunting clothes on before the season, and this won't happen.

Ten: *"The buck must have seen me move when I lifted my gun."*

There are three speeds

If you forget the shooting sticks at home, a tree can help steady your weapon during the moment of truth.

you need for deer hunting. Slow, slower, and slowest. Deer are extremely adept at detecting motion.

Eleven: *"When I clicked off my safety, that buck just exploded."*

Practice in your living room. Any safety can be silently shifted to the off position. Ditto for cocking that hammer on your muzzleloader or old .30-30 lever action.

Twelve: *"The buck was moving and I just couldn't seem to get on him good."*

Hunting rabbits with a scope-sighted .22 rifle or hunting fox and coyotes with a varmint rifle is the best practice for running targets, especially if you miss as many of them standing still as I do! However, since you're probably not going to hunt either, try this:

Make sure your rifle is empty, then practice getting on the birds, squirrels and rabbits flitting and scampering about your backyard. You don't even have to go outside where you might give the neighbor a heart attack; you can do it from inside the house while looking out the window.

Thirteen: *"Man, I got off five rounds faster than you can blink. I don't know how that buck got through all of that lead."*

I do! Firepower is no substitute for accuracy.

Deer scent myths

When it comes to scents, we deer hunters are split down the middle — believers and non-believers. There's a lot of inaccurate information out there about deer scents, and it generates some of skepticism about their use. Call them myths. Here are some of those myths and the real facts on scent use. Understanding them should help you to see more deer and have better deer opportunities this fall.

Myth: The deer scent industry is a hoax. That urine does not even come from deer, but is collected from rabbits, cows, and sheep.

Fact: So far every deer farm I've visited where deer urine is collected had deer, lots of them, and no rabbits, cows, or sheep in sight.

Unscrupulous companies in the scent business don't last. The best advertising in the world for a scent company is when you use their product, have good results with it, then tell your buddy about the product. Without that kind of hunter-to-hunter advertising, a scent company goes belly-up.

Myth: Put on enough cover scent and deer cannot smell you.

Fact: Deer are smart enough to know that

Whenever doctoring a scrape or making a mock scrape, remember to add scent to an overhanging branch via a scent wick.

something that smells like a 200-pound fox sitting up in a tree could be dangerous. Cover scents do not "cover" human odor as their name implies. They help camouflage human odor and confuse deer long enough for you to get a shot. Pay attention to odor control, and you may not need a cover scent.

Myth: Food scents are just as attractive to deer as bait, and it's a lot easier to pour out a little sweet corn scent than to dump a half ton of carrots.

Fact: The second part is true, but the part about food scents being as attractive to deer as a pile of bait is dead wrong. Here is the difference: Deer A is walking through the woods and gets a whiff of those carrots. He follows his nose to the source, fills his belly, and wanders off. The next day and the next and the next (until all of the carrots are gone), Deer A returns to have a few more carrots. That provides you with multiple shot opportunities.

Deer B is walking through the woods and gets a snoot full of that sweet corn scent. He follows his nose to the source of the scent, finds nothing to eat and leaves. Shoot now or forget about seeing him again.

Myth: Deer scents spook deer.

Fact: Human scent spooks deer, not deer scents. I've used at least a 55-gallon drum full of deer scents during the past 25 years, and I can count on one hand the number of deer that have spooked when encountering the scent. In all but one instance, the culprit was a mature doe, the most nervous and "smartest" deer in the woods.

Myth: The best scents are those collected one day and shipped overnight in a refrigerated container. That's the only way to capture those little things called pheromones.

Fact: So far, despite numerous claims to the contrary, nobody has come up with a way to bottle pheromones. Without getting into the chemistry of pheromones, I seriously doubt anyone ever will.

As for fresh scent being better than older scent, the jury is still out. As long as urine smells like urine and not ammonia, which is what is left when the urine gets stale, I've had equal results with off-the-shelf and overnight-fresh scents.

Myth: If you hunt with a decoy, put some deer scent on it to attract more deer.

Fact: You will not attract any more deer to a scented decoy than you will to one without any scent. Scent holds a deer's attention longer once it gets to the decoy, which in turn gives you more opportunity to make the perfect shot.

Speaking of scent and decoys, I no longer put scent directly on the decoy, but instead jab a stick in the ground underneath it and hang a scent wick with a few drops of scent on it.

Myth: When you hike into the woods pulling a drag rag, always drag the rag to one side so that the deer does not smell your tracks.

Fact: If your boots are not odor free, your socks fresh and your feet clean, the deer will smell your human scent trail whether the drag rag is off to one side or over your tracks.

Myth: Synthetic scent is a waste of money. It does not even smell like deer pee.

Fact: Synthetic scents are not supposed to smell like deer urine. Synthetic scents are formulated to appeal to a deer for different reasons. It might be sexual, it may be territorial, it might be dominance, or in many cases — perhaps most — it appeals to a whitetail's curiosity. What's the difference as long as the deer is attracted to the scent?

Myth: All of this business about doctoring scrapes is B.S. I've dumped scent in a bunch of scrapes, and every buck I've seen come to the scrape just worked the overhanging branch and ignored the scrape.

Fact: The main focus of any scrape is the overhanging branch. When a buck licks, chews, rubs his face, or hooks his antlers on the branch, he deposits scent from his pre-orbital, forehead, saliva, and nasal glands. And because a buck frequently licks his urine-stained tarsal glands, he leaves behind the scent of his tarsals and urine on the overhanging branch, too. That's a wealth of information to any other deer visiting the scrape. When you doctor a scrape or make a mock scrape, scenting the overhanging branch by wiring a scent-saturated scent wick to the branch is an important step.

Myth: My Uncle Joe says to get a buck to visit a scrape, urinate in it on your way to the stand.

Fact: Uncle Joe is right. If you pee in a scrape, some deer will probably visit it. The latest controlled study on the subject found that to be the case. What the study did not indicate was how many deer smelled the human urine in the scrape at a distance and avoided it. Nor did the study indicate whether the bucks that visited the scrape containing human urine were curious youngsters or more cautious mature bucks. I'm betting it was the former.

Go ahead and follow Uncle Joe's lead. Me? I'll stick to what I know works and use a bottle for my field toiletry needs, thank you very much.

The scoop on scent-absorbing clothing

S cent-absorbing clothing is no gimmick. The technology is legitimate, and if you use scent-absorbing clothing correctly you'll dramatically decrease the amount of human odor you scatter while hunting.

I've worn scent-absorbing garments while bowhunting deer, and often while hunting with firearms as well, since 1992. That was the year that a Michigan-based chemical engineer named Greg Sesselmann decided that activated charcoal, which had been used for years in other industries, could help control human odor. Greg sent me a stiff, green suit that he said contained activated charcoal between the layers of fabric. He said that industry and the military had used activated charcoal to absorb various organic compounds, which is exactly what human odor is, an organic compound.

Sesselmann's sales pitch sounded a little far-fetched to me, but by 1992 I had begun practicing odor control in my deer hunting, using the odor-reducing powders, sprays, shampoos, and soaps. Using these products already had reduced some odor because my scent had spooked fewer deer

In addition to employing the latest scent-inhibiting clothing, many bowhunters pull on a pair of rubber boots before heading afield.

79

than ever before, but I was still scaring too many. The suit was worth a try.

That first suit was too hot during the early months of the season, too cold in November, and too darn stiff no matter the month. But by the end of that first season, I knew Sesselmann's product, the first Scent-Lok suit, worked.

Scent-Lok is still the "big-hitter" in the world of activated charcoal clothing for hunting, but in recent years, two new players have entered the game. A Minnesota company, Robinson Labs, of Cannon Falls, introduced ScentBlocker a few years back, about the same time that W.L. Gore of Gore-Tex fame, introduced Supprescent. All of the hunting apparel companies that now offer scent-absorbing clothing purchase the material used in their lines from one of these three companies.

I've worn activated-charcoal clothing manufactured by each of the three companies, and none, in my estimation, is superior to the others. There are simply too many variables for me to declare one superior.

For instance, you can find activated-charcoal clothing available in everything from ultra-light clothing for the early season hunter, to heavy-weight outfits for the late-season diehard. The light-weight clothing has less activated charcoal than the mid-weight and heavy-weight versions. The only true test would be to compare activated-charcoal clothing from each manufacturer containing the same amount of activated charcoal per square yard. Such a contest probably would be a draw — all of them getting the job done.

The real question is how will each of these products stand up to the abuse hunters dish out. If you wear an outfit an average of 30 days per season, how many seasons will the suit perform before you will need to purchase a new one? These outfits are not inexpensive, (prices start at about $150) so purchasing a new one each year is not practical for most of us. Supprescent and ScentBlocker haven't been around long enough yet for me to answer that question, but I've worn some Scent-Lok suits for a decade, and near as I (and the deer) can tell, they still perform.

Scent-absorbing clothing has come a long, long way since that first incredibly uncomfortable liner of '92. Today, you can purchase shirts, jackets, parkas, pants, bibs, hoods, face masks, caps, and even boots with scent-absorbing abilities.

Scent-Lok alone now offers a variety of options, including a much-improved and comfortable liner for under your outer layer of clothing. In outerwear, you can choose from a 3-D bushy-leaf camouflage, a very light-weight, cotton outfit for early season hunting, or a quiet, soft micro-denier in either camouflage or blaze orange.

Whether you purchase Supprescent, ScentBlocker, or Scent-Lok, remember this: When used alone, activated charcoal can help decrease the amount of human odor you scatter, but for maximum effectiveness, start with a clean body and use other odor-reducing products such as sprays and powders.

As part of a total odor-control system, activated-charcoal clothing may well be the biggest "edge" any whitetail hunter can have.

EQUIPMENT STRATEGIES
Thoughts on camouflage evolution

I began bowhunting in the late 1960s, took a little time off from deer hunting for hunting of a different sort in a place called Vietnam, then finally took my first deer with stick and string in the fall of 1972.

I did not own a camera at the time and about the only time my family used the old 35mm was at Christmas, Easter, and maybe a baptism or first communion, so I don't have a picture of myself with that first bowhunting trophy.

If one existed, it would show a dark-haired version of myself proudly lifting the head of that whitetail doe with one hand and clutching a Herter's solid-glass recurve with the other.

Now, ask me what I wore yesterday, and I couldn't tell you. But I can share with you exactly what I wore that late October afternoon nearly 30 years past. Nancy Clancy might just have something when she asserts that I possess "selective memory."

Over a pair of cotton long underwear, I wore a flannel shirt and a gray, hooded sweatshirt. My pants were Carhartt bib overalls in the same brown color as you see on today's Carhartts. Over a mop of unruly hair, most of which remains along the trail, was a Jones-style duck hunter's cap in the same brown color as the bibs.

My feet wore an old pair of oft-patched hip-boots, not because I was worried about odor control, but because I had to cross a creek to reach my stand. A year or two later, when I found a set of tiger-stripe Army-issue jungle fatigues like those worn by Recon, Ranger, and Special Forces units in 'Nam, I was the envy of every other bowhunter in Freeborn County — all two or three dozen of us back then. Nobody wore camouflage in those days.

Today, I don't know a single bowhunter who doesn't wear camouflage. Blame Bill Jordan for that. Yeah, I know that Jim Crumley introduced his Trebark camouflage prior to Bill Jordan's Realtree and that there were various versions of the so-called "woodland" camo around, but it was Jordan who devised the marketing campaign destined to convince every bowhunter (and turkey hunter, small game hunter, and waterfowler, too) that without camouflage, he might just as well stay at home.

Most people view Jordan as a television and video celebrity on his Realtree Outdoors television show and Monster Bucks video series. What most don't know is that Bill is also one keen businessman. Realtree Camouflage clothing is worn by more hunters than any other brand of camo and is now found on everything from ATVs to toilet paper. Realtree has grown into a larger company than Bill ever dreamed.

Toxey Haas and his Mossy Oak camouflage is the other "big player" in the camouflage world. Both Realtree and Mossy Oak are available in a variety of different patterns, and every year or so each company introduces a new pattern. There are a number of smaller camouflage companies such as Predator, Skyline, and others. And each year, a handful of new companies test the camouflage waters, find them too hot, and disappear.

Many years ago, when Bill Jordan and Realtree were not household names among the hunting crowd, Jordan invited me and some other hunting writers to Georgia to hunt deer with him. We all wore his camouflage, and when we took "grip-and-grin" photos of each other with our bucks, guess what we wore? Bill devoted the lion's share of his modest advertising budget during the early years to such hunts, believing (as it turned out, correctly) that the photos we would publish of hunters dressed in Realtree was more vital to his success than the advertising he could purchase. Other companies followed his lead.

Few features are as distinctive in the woods as the human face. To avoid letting your mug spook deer, wear a camo face mask or apply camo makeup liberally.

Bottom line: Today there is a mind-boggling number of camouflage patterns from which to choose. How do you decide which is best?

First, forget the notion and disregard the advertisements that claim that camouflage X is the end-all of camouflage and is as effective in September as in December. T'ain't so.

In the Upper Midwest, we start bowhunting the middle of September while the woods remain decked out in late-summer greenery with a smattering of browns, reds, and yellow. By Halloween the same woods are a drab, colorless place with naked trees, brush and forest floor all fitting under the basic coloration of gray/brown. Then, when December comes, unless El Niño rules once again, our world turns white.

No single camouflage pattern will allow you to "blend in" under those three radically different conditions. At the least you will need two, one that suffices for the early season and the mid-season, and another for when snow has fallen.

Any of the Realtree or Mossy Oak patterns, or those from lesser-known companies will work for early and mid-season. My personal preference is for "open" patterns. Realtree's Advantage Timber or Mossy Oak Break-Up are both excellent. Open patterns diffuse or blur the human outline better than darker patterns. That's also why I like those 3-D leafy suits.

Then get yourself some snow camouflage or a set of whites. I usually wear a set of whites for predator hunting. They are made by a small company in Alberta called Ravenwear. They are fleece and very quiet.

Camouflage allows us to move a little more than if dressed in regular duds. Dressed in a suit of passionate pink (OK, I won't wear that!) I could visit the woods, and as long as I sit still, deer will not see me. Move, however, even just to lift my binoculars to my eyes, scratch an itch, eat a candy bar, or draw my bow, and odds are the whitetail's motion-sensitive eyes will pick me off. Dressed in camouflage (instead of that pink), I can justify those movements.

And you must camouflage hands and face. Both are pale, likely to be moving and spooky to deer. Use either a face mask or make-up variety from a tube.

For maximum effectiveness, regardless of what brand or pattern of camo you wear, remember these three tips.

- Use tree limbs, brush, leaves, grass, cornstalks, or anything around you to help break up your outline. If you skyline or silhouette yourself, it won't matter what camo you wear; deer will spot you.

- Whenever possible, stick to the shadows. Ever notice how much more difficult a deer is to see when he's in deep shadow instead of highlighted by the sun? That applies to you and I, too.

- You can't buy the best camouflage at any store. The ability to sit still for long periods and move only in slow motion when movement is necessary can be learned by any hunter.

Deer hunting via muzzleloader

B ack in the early 1970s, I heard about something called a "special muzzleloader season" being held at the Ft. McCoy Military Reservation near Sparta, Wis. I did not own a muzzleloader and had never even shot one, but I was already a nut about white-tailed deer, so I borrowed a .50 Thompson/Center Hawken from my brother-in-law, John Carlin, the only person I knew at the time who owned a muzzleloader. John showed me how to load, shoot, and clean that heavy hunk of iron, and on opening morning I slipped up on a sleek buck and two does as they scarfed down acorns, drew a bead on the buck, and when the smoke cleared, there lay that buck, stone-cold-dead.

In the almost 30 years since that morning on that Wisconsin ridge, a lot of things have changed in the world of muzzleloading for white-tailed deer. That "special muzzleloader season" that was so special back then is now commonplace. Most states and provinces have a season just for the blackpowder enthusiast. The guns, bullets, powders, and primers have changed, too, mostly for the better. During those years of hunting with a muzzleloader, I made a lot of mistakes. I thought I might share some of them with you, so you won't make them, too.

• When you sight in that muzzleloader, have it strike dead-on at somewhere between 75 and 100 yards. I once sighted in everything for two or three inches high at 100, figuring I would have a better chance of connecting with that long shot of 125 or even 150 yards. The problem with this faulty reasoning is twofold. One, most opportunities at white-tailed deer up here in our part of the country are at ranges well under 100 yards, so it makes sense to be right-on-the-money at the ranges you are likely to encounter a deer. And two, most of us exaggerate the range and hold a little high to compensate. When your rifle impacts a couple inches high at 100 yards, guess where that bullet goes when that deer is standing 50 yards away? You guessed it: sailing harmlessly right over the deer's back.

• Many of the modern in-line muzzleloaders are now beefed up to handle charges of 150 grains of powder. The whole idea behind the hefty powder charge is more speed from the projectile. The faster that bullet travels when it leaves the muzzle, the better the trajectory downrange. The concept works. I've shot hundreds of rounds through various muzzleloaders with 150-grain powder charges (three 50-grain Pyrodex Pellets) and when you get out on the far side of the 100-yard marker, the heavy charge holds the advantage over a lesser charge. But I've found that you pay for that flatter trajectory at the shoulder and in accuracy. Invariably, regardless of the rifle, I obtain my best accuracy with powder charges from 90 to 120 grains.

• Shoot a good bullet. Whether you shoot a conical bullet or a saboted bullet, there are lots of premium projectiles, and believe me, the quality of the projectile you send screaming down that tube is more important than the brand name on the barrel of the rifle. A quality muzzleloader bullet is designed specifically for muzzleloading, meaning the bullet is designed for controlled expansion, superior penetration, and weight retention at the velocities attained with muzzle-loading rifles. I've taken deer with conicals from Thompson/Center, Hornady, and Buffalo Bullets and have been pleased with the results of all of them.

Whitetailers should sight their muzzleloader in for between 75 and 100 yards. In the Upper Midwest, most of your shots will occur at that range or less.

For the past 10 years, I've hunted

exclusively with saboted bullets. A sabot is a plastic sleeve that holds the projectile and imparts spin to the projectile on the short trip down the barrel. Shortly after exiting the muzzle, the plastic sabot falls away and the projectile continues on to the target. The beauty of a saboted bullet is that you can shoot a lighter bullet that makes for a flatter trajectory. I've had excellent results with the Barnes Expander MZ, Nosler and Swift A-Frame saboted bullets over the years. This year I'm shooting the new Winchester Partition Gold 260-grain saboted bullet and have been very pleased with the performance.

•When the old mountain men met once a year for what they called a rendezvous, their salutation to each other when saying good-bye when the party was over was to "keep your powder dry." That same salutation should be your battle cry. Blackpowder and Pyrodex tend not to ignite if damp, and I can tell you from sad, personal experience, that having hunted hard for a good shot, only to have the powder fail to ignite at the moment of truth is a sickening feeling.

Most of the time the culprit is not rain or snow, but condensation. If you're hunting in cold weather and bring the rifle into a warm vehicle or building, condensation will form on the cold metal. If that condensation reaches your powder charge, and it probably will, all you'll hear at the moment of truth is a sickening click! When it's cold out, unless I'm going to clean the rifle and start with a new load in the morning, I do not bring the rifle into the heat.

•Speaking of cleaning, my rule for a muzzleloader is this: If you shoot it today, clean it today. If you do not, you can ruin the rifle. The residue left behind by both black powder and Pyrodex is extremely hygroscopic, which means that it will literally pull moisture right out of the air. The corrosion process begins as soon as you pull the trigger. On hunting trips and in camp, I use pre-saturated patches to swab out the barrel. Once home I give the barrel a good scrubbing with hot water and liquid dishwashing detergent. I ruined a good rifle once because I failed to clean it for several days after firing several rounds through it. And no, just because your rifle happens to have a stainless steel barrel will not save it from corrosion.

•One last tip. At the range, practice re-loading quickly. With a little practice, you should be able to reload in less than 30 seconds. Then, when hunting, get in the habit of reloading quickly after you shoot, especially if the deer drops in its tracks. A deer that goes down like a hammer is often struck close enough to the spinal column to momentarily paralyze the animal, but if the shot is not fatal, the deer will regain its senses and run.

This habit has saved me several deer over the years, including the second largest buck I've ever taken.

A case for
the .30-06

My father-in-law, The Old Scutter, and most of my other friends think I get most of my guns for free. I wish!

The truth of the matter is that while outdoors writers can purchase most firearms at a discount, it's rare that we receive guns as gifts. That is why, a few years back, when I was invited on a deer hunt to southeast Colorado by the folks at Browning Arms, I was surprised and tickled to learn that the rifle we chose for the hunt would be ours to keep. The rifle, a shiny new Browning A-Bolt with the then-new BOSS configuration was available in several calibers, including a couple of the hot .30-caliber magnums that have become so popular during my lifetime. But when Travis Hall, the Browning representative called to ask me what caliber of rifle I would like, my answer was simple. "I'll take a .30-06."

When it comes to rifle hunting for whitetails, and most other North American big game, you'll likely find the author toting the reliable .30-06.

Nostalgia had something to do with my choice. Like many of you, my first rifle was a sporterized .30-06 Springfield. That rifle might have been carried by a soldier in any of the three major wars in which the Springfield served this country's servicemen so well. With a new walnut stock, a blue job, and a Williams peep sight, I turned it into a "deer rifle."

Hundreds of thousands of other hunters did the same. Surplus Springfields were cheap back then.

But you can't explain the continued popularity of the .30-06 simply by nostalgia or the once endless supply of inexpensive military surplus rifles. The days of walking into a sporting goods store and finding a barrel stuffed with Springfields with a sign reading "Take Your Pick For $20" are history. No, the .30-06 remains the favorite caliber with America's deer hunters for a better reason: It does the job.

Number crunchers will say that the .30-06 is ballistically inferior to many cartridges available today. The numbers don't lie. But white-tailed deer do not spend much time reading ballistic charts. A whitetail does not care if that 150-grain, factory-loaded .30-06 bullet is only capable of 2,900 feet per second (fps); if the 165-grain pill tops out at 2,800 fps; or if the ever-popular 180-grain chugs along at barely 2,700 fps. Of course those who handload know they can easily and dramatically exceed the factory round numbers, but again, Mr. Whitetail is not impressed.

Call me old fashioned, but I have not run into a situation in the deer woods where I needed more range or more knock-'em-down-and-keep-'em-down power than the .30-06 delivers.

Although I personally prefer a bolt-action rifle, I like that the .30-06 is available in every action conceivable. And while the .30-06 is no cream-puff in either category, neither muzzle blast nor recoil is excessive. I also take a certain measure of comfort in knowing that if I should ever need a box of .30-06 ammo in some remote location, odds are good that I can find a box at the local country store. If I forget to pack my ammunition for deer camp, chances are two or three of the other hunters will have a spare box or two of .30-06 ammo. Try that with your .366 Nitro-Blaster Express.

This is a white-tailed deer hunting book, but I must address the versatility of the .30-06. Legend has it that even Jack

O'Connor, the champion of the .270 Winchester, privately con-
ceded that the .30-06 was more versatile than his beloved .270
Winchester. If this fall, or the next, or the next, I traipse off to
Alaska, Newfoundland, or British Columbia for caribou, it is
the .30-06 you will find missing from my gun case. Ditto for
elk. Black bear, too. While the .30-06 might be more gun than
you need for the thin-skinned pronghorn, the ought-six is
long enough, flat enough, and fast enough to handle the job
on these prairie speedsters. And if I live long enough to draw
a Minnesota moose tag, I'll tote it then, too. While I would
consider other calibers for long-range sheep hunting, some
Africa game, or an encounter with the bears bigger than our
blacks, I also would not feel under-gunned carrying a .30-06.

I leave you with this bit of my own deer hunting history. The
first deer I ever shot with that old sporterized .30-06
Springfield was a big doe feeding along the edge of a gnarly
swamp up in what they used to call "The Gulch Country"
west of Walker, Minn.

There was 40 square miles of roadless country at the time
and few hunters reached the middle of it. The doe was about
75 yards away when I took a good rest up alongside a popple
tree, peered through that rear aperture, settled the front blade
on her shoulder, thumbed off that big safety, and nudged the
trigger. The rifle bucked and the deer dropped. I spent the rest
of the day dragging that doe to the nearest logging road.

The last deer I shot with a .30-06 was a big 8-pointer that
jumped from his hiding place in a nasty patch of scrub willow
and tried to put some distance between himself and the guy in
orange bold enough to invade his hidey-hole. The angle on
the running buck was severe so I purposefully put that round
just in front of his right hind leg and let the 165-grain bullet
plow forward through his vitals. Sounds gruesome, but I hope
that when my time is up, I go as fast as that buck. He died
mid-stride. When I skinned him out, I found the perfectly
mushroomed bullet just under the hide of his off shoulder.

Going back through the pages of my memory, on every hunt
that I carried a .30-06 into the deer woods, I cannot recall a
single instance where a second shot was needed to anchor a
deer. A few deer ran a short ways before collapsing, but most
simply dropped where they had stood.

I rest my case.

Slugs: You've come a long way baby!

My first "slug gun" was a Model 1897 Winchester 12 gauge pump. Its 32-inch barrel had a full choke that was just fine for heaving an ounce-and-a quarter of chilled No. 4s at high-flying mallards or rooster pheasants jumping up ahead of a half-broke hunting dog. But man oh man, that old cornsheller was something else when it came to shooting those one-ounce hunks of lead that we call slugs.

Probably because the choke was so tight on that barrel, the old '97 tended to spray slugs like a runaway firehose. One might be a foot high, another a foot low and off to the left. It's hard to compensate for such fickleness. Back in the days before rifled barrels and saboted slugs, shotgun-toting deer hunters were accustomed to compensating for the lack of accuracy that smooth bores, tight chokes, and the old Foster-style slugs produced.

Uncle Jerry, The Old Scutter's baby brother, had a Model 50 Winchester semi-auto that actually grouped

Today's sabot-shooting, rifle-barrel-toting deer hunter can shoot accurately twice as far as the old smoothbore deer hunters of 30 years ago.

93

slugs pretty well at 50 yards. As long as Jerry could remember to hold six inches high and nearly a foot to the right, to compensate for the Model 50's habit of shooting six inches low and a foot to the left, he did OK. When I got tired of missing deer with my long-barreled pump, I picked up another old pump, sold by Sears sometime back in the 1920s, and took it to a gunsmith by the name of Bob Kaplan who had a shop in the back of Berglund's Sporting Goods in Albert Lea, Minn.

Bob would ream that choke a tad and I would fire a few slugs through the gun, then bring it back for a touch more reaming. When Bob was finished working on that old pump I had me a deer-killing machine. Never mind that the barrel was 30 inches long and the only "sight" was the little gold bead on the end of the barrel. At 50 yards I could send a three-pound coffee can spinning across the gravel pit with every shot from my "new slug gun."

Sounds silly today, but back then that was pretty impressive shooting. That old pump and I made some miles up and down the hills of the Whitewater Wildlife Management Area and accounted for a bunch of deer in our camp through the years. Of course the gun was old and half wore out when I bought it for $20, so I guess it's not surprising that I retired that old pump when it developed the nasty habit of occasionally going off on its own when I slammed a fresh slug home. There's a habit that unless you happen to have the nervous system of a Holstein, will almost always result in a severe case of flinching.

Of course there were a few so-called "slug guns" available back then, most notably the Ithaca Model 37 Deerslayer. Later, Remington introduced a short-barreled version of its Model 870 for deer hunters. These slug guns featured short barrels and adjustable sights, and while they were certainly a big improvement over what most of us toted, they were a far cry from today's modern slug guns.

The revolution in slug guns occurred with the nearly simultaneous development of the sabot slug and the rifled shotgun barrels designed to shoot them accurately. There are still hunters who scoff at sabot slugs, claiming that they aren't even as accurate as the old-style Foster slugs many of us grew up shooting. This is often true when we fire saboted slugs through smooth bores as opposed to rifled barrels. Generally, barrels without rifling will shoot the old style slugs better — often much better than the saboted slugs. But marry a saboted slug to a rifled slug barrel, and you have a deadly combination.

A sabot is nothing more than a plastic cup or sleeve that holds the projectile, much like a shot cup or plastic wad holds the pellets in a shotgun shell. In the case of pellets, the big advantage to the plastic wad (cup) is that it prevents the pellets from making contact with the barrel and deforming, which leads to poor patterns.

But the plastic sabot serves an entirely different purpose. When you pull the trigger on your shotgun, several things happen quickly. The primer detonates, which ignites the powder. The resulting explosion causes the plastic sabot to expand so that the rifling grips it tightly. The rifling imparts spin to the sabot, which in turn imparts spin to the slug encased in the sabot. This spin keeps the slug on course once it exits the barrel and the sabot falls away. The result: better accuracy.

Trajectory also has improved because the projectile in the sabot is lighter than the big hunk of lead in the old-style shotgun slug, and manufacturers have worked to improve velocity. This doesn't mean that a shotgun slug is now a formidable long-range projectile. It is not. But with practice, you can put that slug in the boilers of a buck at 100 yards or slightly beyond without resorting to the equivalent of football's Hail Mary pass.

Today every shotgun manufacturer features guns specifically designed for shooting slugs. You can choose from semi-automatics, pumps, bolt action, or single shots. You can spend a couple hundred bucks or plunk down a grand. Most slug guns come with adjustable open sights, but most hunters prefer to mount a scope on their slug gun. I've never met anyone who could shoot better with open sights than with a scope. A straight power 2.5X or 4X will do nicely, or you can go with a low power variable-power scope, with something in the 1.5-5X ideally suited to the slug gun.

One more thing: Many 12-gauge slug guns kick like the proverbial mule. This is especially true in pump-action, single-shot, and bolt-action models. Semi-autos tend to be a little more gentle on the butt end because the action absorbs some of the recoil as it ejects the spent casing and feeds a new round into the chamber. Young hunters or those of small frame will likely shoot better with a 20 gauge than with a 12 gauge, and the slight decrease in "knockdown punch" between the 12 and the 20 will more than off-set their ability to shoot accurately.

It's an old, worn-out cliche, but when it comes to slugs and slug guns, we've come a long way baby!

Gearing up
for bowhunting

Followers of my Strictly Whitetails writing know I focus mostly on sharing hunting stories and technique. I steer away from technical material on equipment because I'm not a very technical guy. In fact, when it comes to tools and figuring out how things are supposed to work, I'm a real klutz. That probably makes you wonder why I'm penning this piece on gear for bowhunting. Well, that's the reason. That I'm an admitted klutz, I mean.

The great news for me, and for all of those of you who are like me, is that you can shoot a bow as well as the next guy and never understand how those wheels, cams, cables, and strings all work together to launch that arrow on the straight and narrow. You can be as deadly as old Fred Bear and not have a clue as to how to figure kinetic energy.

If you have no interest, you need never learn how to fletch an arrow, glue a nock, or replace a string. Like me, you may be comfortable leaving that stuff to the experts and devoting your energies to learning about whitetails instead.

Staff at your local archery pro shop can make the sometimes complex world of modern bowhunting much more understandable for the beginner.

97

Thanks to steady and dramatic improvement in archery equipment since the introduction of the compound bow in the late 1960s, today literally anyone can, with the right equipment, the proper instruction, and some practice, be shooting surprisingly well in a short time.

The compound bow reaches its peak holding weight prior to full draw, and at full draw the holding weight drops off anywhere from 50 to 85 percent depending upon the bow. This makes it possible to comfortably hold a bow at full draw with plenty of time to aim and release. This more than any factor is responsible for attracting legions of new hunters to the sport of bowhunting, and it's the main reason why the sport has attracted more women hunters and youngsters in recent years.

As is the case with any new invention, the first generation of compound bows had a few bugs. One of the biggest problems always has been keeping the bow in tune. In simple terms, this means making sure that the wheels, cams, cable, and the string all work in unison. If they do not, then the bow is out of tune and accuracy is impossible.

Mathew McPherson, the brain trust behind Mathews Archery, virtually eliminated that problem a few years back with the introduction of the now common single-cam technology. I wouldn't say that single-cam bows have eliminated the problem of bows getting out of tune, but it's very rare to hear of a single-cam bow in need of a tune-up.

But let's get right to the really, really good news. Without knowing anything about archery other than you would like to try it, you can walk into an archery pro shop, explain your situation to the archery staffer, and he or she will take it from there. Working within your budget, the archery pro will fit you with a bow that features the proper draw weight and length, help you select the proper arrows for your bow, install a rest, sight, and peep sight on your bow, and recommend several good releases aids.

OK, I can see the wheels churning for some of you now. You are saying to yourself, "Hey, I can buy all of this stuff out of a catalog and save myself a bundle." Sure you will save yourself a few dollars by going the mail order route, but you are going to buy yourself a bunch of headaches. Unless you're really good at setting up a bow, go the archery shop route when getting started.

Now that you have the equipment, an archery pro can help you learn to use it. Resist the urge to just go off by yourself and start flinging arrows. All you will do is develop bad habits. Take a couple of lessons from the pro and then follow his instructions. You will be shooting like a champ in short order and on your way to a lifetime of enjoyment.

Welcome aboard!

Thoughts on modern treestands

It was back in the early 1970s. I was hunting deer with the Boughten Bunch in Minnesota's Whitewater Wildlife Management Area, having finally been officially invited after marrying the lovely Nancy Boughten. The Boughten Bunch had this unwritten rule that said no boyfriends could participate in the hunt. They were worried that some tall, young Irishman from Albert Lea, Minn., would be so brazen as to feign love just for the opportunity to hunt the place they simply called "The Deer Valley."

Anyway, I've always referred to ours as a "shotgun wedding" because of the circumstances just described. But I digress....

It was the third day of the season, and I was still-hunting on top of a ridge when I saw another hunter attempting the same thing. I say "attempting" because I could hear him crunching leaves and brush 100 yards away. He had about as much chance of slipping up on an unsuspecting whitetail as does a runaway Sherman tank.

Since the noisy hunter was working my direction, I sat down on a stump and waited for him, thinking that he might just dislodge a deer between us. The ridge I was prowling along was above the sidehill where my brother-in-law Larry usually hunted.

Larry is a good sitter, which means that when he plunks his butt down in a good spot, he sits there all day without moving, which is something few hunters can handle. Larry had shot at a lot of deer over the years off that sidehill stand. When I came on board, I convinced Larry that we should sit in trees instead of on the ground.

Larry figured it made sense when I explained to him that the deer were less likely to see, hear, or smell us while we sat in trees, so he found an old oak with spreading branches, climbed up, and made himself at home. As far as I know, the two of us were the only hunters sitting in trees in that whole valley back then, although there may have been others I did not see.

The noisy hunter walked out onto one of those limestone outcroppings that are common in southeast Minnesota, hoping I suppose, to surprise any deaf deer snoozing below him. Of course any deer bedded within a quarter mile of that outcropping was long gone by the time Old Stumble Foot stepped out onto the edge and peered down into the timber below.

He didn't see any deer, but he saw Larry sitting in that tree. He stood there for a few minutes, smoked a cigarette, then tromped in my direction. The noisy one was within 30 yards before he saw me, but when he did, he marched right over and in a voice better suited for calling signals at Packer-Viking game, asked if I had seen any deer.

Before I could even answer he bellowed, "You know, I saw the darndest thing off that rock back there. A guy sitting in a tree. And he has been in that tree all three days I've hunted here. What'cha suppose he's doing sitting in a tree?"

I looked the noisy one in the eye and in a low voice oozing as much sympathy as I could muster, I tapped my trigger finger on my right temple a couple of times and said, "Yes, I know, that's my brother-in-law. He's not quite playing with a full deck, if you know what I mean."

Perhaps as much as the compound bow and sabot slug, the modern treestand has revolutionized white-tailed deer hunting during the past 25 years.

He appeared stunned for a few moments, then nodded his head slowly up and down, as if he had just come to some great revelation, and said, "Uh-huh, I thought it was probably something like that."

Back then, many hunters considered sitting in a tree to hunt deer strange behavior. Today, most deer hunters spend a good share of their time in the woods perched in treestands. The reason for hunting from trees is the same as it has always been: The deer are less likely to detect you if you're perched above them instead of on their level. And in most cases, deer are much easier to see from an elevated position than they are from ground level.

Hunting from a treestand is a bigger advantage for the bowhunter than for a firearms hunter because the archer must have the deer close for the shot and draw the arrow without being detected. But whatever my weapon, I usually hunt from a treestand.

Back when I started hunting from trees, the tree itself was the stand. The trick was to find a tree with branches horizontal enough that you could sit or stand on them, usually using the trunk of the tree for a brace or backrest. Like Larry, I often spent an entire day perched in the branches of some gnarly white oak. At the time, I don't remember thinking much of it. Some hunters who hunted on private land would nail a two-by-four, or two, across a couple of branches and balance or sit on the boards.

In the past 20 years, treestands have become so common that just the idea of climbing a tree and perching on the branches sounds ridiculous. I can remember my first real treestand and how it felt to stand on the platform and sit in that comfortable seat. Compared to sitting or standing on a branch all day, it was like trading up from a '61 Falcon to a decked-out Cadillac Coupe Deville.

If memory serves (and it likely may not) the first commercial treestand was a climbing model introduced by a company called Amacker. Climbing stands never have been very popular up here in our part of the country, but I've got one and use it a dozen times a season. There are times when a climber makes more sense than a fixed-position stand. The only real drawback to a climbing stand is that they won't work on a tree with a bunch of branches.

But there are plenty of maples, basswoods, and even straight oaks that lend themselves well to a climber with only the need to trim a couple of small branches as you ascend. Aspens, the ones some of us call popples, are perfectly suited to a climber.

Climbers are no longer big, clumsy, noisy, and unsafe. That has all changed. Today a good climber is first and foremost safe, easy to latch to the tree, and quiet. A climber is fast, too. No screwing in steps or lashing climbing sticks to a tree and then hanging a stand. Just fasten the climber to the tree, hop aboard, and climb.

Which brings me to another thing I like about climbers. With a climber it's easy to go another five or even 10 feet up. I can't remember the last time a deer picked me off while I hunted from a climber. The biggest reason: I commonly hunt 25 or even 30 feet in the air. Even deer accustomed to looking up for danger rarely look that high.

Some hunters claim that a climbing stand is more dangerous than a fixed-position stand. Actually, the opposite is true, because with a climber, you attach yourself to the tree via a safety harness during the ascent and the descent, which is when most falls take place.

All that said, however, most of the time I hunt from a fixed-position stand. On private land where it's permissible to leave stands overnight, I have most of my stands hung well before the deer season. A fixed-position stand will work on any tree large enough to hold you, regardless of limb configuration. A well-made, fixed-position stand is safe, solid, noise-free, easy to install, and comfortable, even for the all-day sit. A poorly made fixed-position stand is noisy, uncomfortable, and potentially unsafe. Don't trim your hunting budget in the treestand department.

Ladder stands are becoming more popular. Part of the reason for this upsurge in popularity, I believe, is because more and more hunters are buying or leasing land for deer hunting. A ladder stand ideally is suited for those who want to put up a stand once and leave it there. In fact, I would suggest that the longer you leave a ladder stand in one place, the better the odds that you will see deer at close range from that stand.

I have two ladder stands in place on a farm, and even though I put them up a month before the bow season, the deer did not really accept them as part of the landscape that first season.

One is back in the timber, but the other is on the edge of an alfalfa field, and every deer that stepped out into that alfalfa field to feed in the evening would stop and watch that ladder stand. Those old, fussy does were the worst.

The farmer lets me leave my stands in place during the off-season, and with ladder stands, I do. By the second season the deer had accepted the ladder stands as part of the landscape, and I routinely saw them at close range from both ladder stands. For gun hunting, where getting up close and personal with the deer is not crucial, you can probably set up a ladder stand and hunt from it the same day, but for the bowhunter who intends to use a ladder stand, my experience suggests you are better off getting that stand in position well before the season. Then, the deer have time to become accustomed to it.

Deer decoying tips

Using a deer decoy can add excitement to your bowhunting and might help you attract that monster buck. Let me share with you what has worked for me through the years with a decoy. Remember, however, there is plenty of room to be innovative when it comes to this relatively new deer hunting concept. If you think something sounds off the wall, but might work, don't be bashful, give it a try.

Safety is number one when it comes to using a deer decoy. I have a very simple rule: Never use a decoy when a firearms season is in progress.

Realism

A friend of mine had the most realistic deer decoy I'd ever seen. Tom tanned a deer hide and stretched it over a 3-D deer target. He screwed on a set of 130-class antlers and installed glass eyes. Wake up from a little cat-nap to find that decoy

The art of deer decoying remains a relatively new science. Depending on the status of the breeding season, experiment with different combinations of single decoys, or multiple set ups of bucks and does.

standing at 20 yards and your heart jumps right to your throat. A lot of bucks came to that decoy though it was a pain to lug around the woods.

On the other side of the coin, I've seen bucks respond to some pretty crude homemade silhouette decoys.

When a buck is really hot, I believe realism doesn't matter. But, if the buck is one of those suspicious critters, then realism can make the difference.

Buck, doe or both?

Most of the time, I use a buck decoy. There is a three- to five-day period in late October when the bucks are really chasing does, but if the does are not ready to breed, I take off the antlers and transform my deer decoy into a doe. If hauling the decoys to the stand was not a hassle, I would lean towards a buck-and-doe combo for every situation. You cover all of the bases when using this combination.

Scent

Many good hunters do not bother with scent on decoys, but I always use scent. When using a buck decoy, I apply a tarsal gland scent on the rear of the decoy or if I have one, I will wire a fresh tarsal gland to the leg of the decoy. When using a doe decoy, I use a doe-in-estrus scent. The scent probably does not help attract deer to the decoy, but I'm convinced that the scent helps hold them around the fake deer longer. The more time a buck spends inspecting and sniffing the decoy, the more opportunities he will present for a good broadside or quartering-away shot. And even though I always wear rubber gloves when handling a decoy, I like to spray the decoy with an odor neutralizer before I apply the scent. You can't be too careful when it comes to fooling a buck's nose.

Movement

If you're a waterfowl hunter, you know that ducks can be very difficult to decoy when the blocks are sitting on the mirror-calm surface on a windless day. Add just enough breeze to sway the decoys on their tethers and the mallards accept them as the real thing.

The same is often true when decoying white-tailed deer. Movement is very often the difference. Decoy manufacturers are aware of the importance of movement and have devised some ingenious devices for adding motion to deer decoys. Take the silhouette deer decoy from Higdon as an example. You pull a string to move the tail or raise the head from the feeding to the alert position.

I once used a decoy that had a tiny, battery-operated motor and a timer you could set so that the tail would wag at intervals. When hunting on the move during the rut, I like to use a folding silhouette decoy. When I set up to rattle, I prop the decoy in front of me and kneel behind it. When a buck approaches and spots that motionless decoy, it will freeze and stare suspiciously at the smaller-than-life silhouette. I take my hands and gently rock or shimmy the decoy to give it movement. You can read the deer as it accepts the decoy as the real thing.

Many hunters use strips of toilet paper on the ears and tail of full-bodied decoys. Toilet paper will flutter in the slightest breeze, but I've found a better alternative to toilet paper, which gets wet and then sticks to the decoy. I cut three 1-inch-wide by 4-inch-long strips from a white plastic garbage bag. The cheap ones, which are only .74 mm, are best because they sway seductively in even the slightest breeze. To attach them to my full body decoy, I use a small finishing nail. Heat the nail with a match or lighter, and the point of the nail melts easily through the plastic strip and the decoy.

Set up

Position the decoy 15 to 25 yards upwind of your stand. Most bucks will attempt to circle the decoy to get downwind, and you want to leave enough room between the stand and the decoy for them to accomplish this — without getting downwind of your position. Never have the decoy facing in your direction. Deer look where other deer are looking just to understand their interest, and there's no sense in encouraging them to look in your direction.

Hunting with a decoy is fun and very exciting. Use these tips to get the most out of your time spent hunting over a deer decoy.

HUNTING TALES

Of hawks
and owls

While bowhunting down at my buddy Jeff Louderback's place during the week of Thanksgiving 2001, I had another hair-raising and very nearly "hair-lifting" experience with a bird of prey. After this episode, I got to thinking about all of the other times I've had similar experiences with hawks and owls and thought you might enjoy hearing about them.

This time, I was in a treestand in a gnarly cottonwood tree and had been in the stand since well before first light. It was my favorite time of the day — plenty light enough to shoot, but not yet sunrise, and I was intent on scanning the timber and grass of the Cimmaron River bottom for any hint of movement that might betray a white-tailed deer. Of all of the places I have ever hunted, a whitetail can appear and disappear in one of those Kansas bottoms quicker than anywhere.

It was a fairly warm morning, so as is my habit, I had my Scent-Lok hood on but instead of having it pulled down over my face,

Spend enough time in a treestand and you'll likely encounter more than one curious, and often hungry, hawk or owl.

I had it tucked up over my ears so that I could hear better. Then when I'd spot a deer headed my way, I'd just reach up and pull the full face mask into position. The way I had the face mask shoved up on my head probably exposed a bit of my gray hair, and that white hair is what caught the eye of the sharp-shinned hawk just cruising along, hunting the river bottom that morning.

The sharp-shinned hawk is not very large, but is a real speedster that feeds mainly on rodents and small birds, many of which it plucks right out of the air. I suspect the hawk was either flying by or perched in a snag as I turned my head slowly from side to side to scan the woods, and my exposed gray hair caught its attention. Whatever the hawk mistook my gray hair for, it must have looked like something worth eating, and the hawk swooped in for the kill.

Lucky for me, hawks aim a tad high. Instead of sinking its talons into my scalp, the hawk got its talons tangled in my face mask. I felt the strike on the back of my head, then one of the hawk's wings slapped me on the side of the face. In an instant, it was over, the hawk swooping away, the hood dangling from its feet, and one gray-haired hunter sitting in a tree with his heart stuck somewhere under his Adam's apple.

That episode reminded me of the time years ago when my old Labrador, Jack Daniels, and I were duck hunting. I threw out the decoys that cold, late October morning in a little slough off Lower Walnut Lake near Blue Earth, Minn., then tucked the duck boat back in the cattails to wait for shooting light. I was younger then, and sometimes burned the midnight oil, so as usual, I suppose, I was a bit bleary-eyed.

With 15 minutes until shooting time, I sat on my old shooting box, hunched over half asleep. Jack sat on the forward deck of the little boat hoping that one of the muskrats swimming among the decoys would venture near so he could launch one of his impressive, but always ineffective, muskrat attacks.

It was cold that morning and I was wearing an old Korean War U.S. Army surplus cap, the kind with the pile lining that you can either fold up and tie on top of the cap, or drape down to cover your ears and neck. I had the lining tied up that morning, and I imagine the cap looked just like a muskrat to that great-horned owl. All of a sudden I felt a whump on top of my head. I let out a huge scream that scared old Jack so bad he fell off the boat.

Scared that owl, too, because it let go of my cap and dropped it out near the decoys. As long as Jack was in the water, I tried to convince him to retrieve the slowly sinking cap, but every time I sent him out he brought back another decoy instead of the cap. A good retriever always brings back something....

A pair of great-horned owls attacked me another time, but that was my own fault. I wanted to get pictures of the baby owls in the nest, so I climbed up a nearby tree hoping to get high enough to shoot photos into the nest from above. The parents did not think much of my photo op. The first one hit me on the right side of my face, and had I not been wearing glasses, I might have lost an eye. As I tried to hold onto the tree, the other parent swooped in and nailed me on the other side of my face. See, those really are not wrinkles of age on this pretty mug of mine, they are scars from losing battles with owls!

Another time, a goshawk — one of only two I have ever seen in Minnesota — nearly knocked me out cold. I was sitting in my treestand bowhunting near Lanesboro and dressed completely in camouflage. I had a face mask pulled down over my head so that only my eyes showed. A goshawk, a large accipiter that's very fast and agile in the woods, made a dive at a bunch of starlings roosted in a nearby cedar tree, but he missed. The birds flushed as one with an audible whoosh, then landed right back in the same tree.

A minute later the goshawk, displaying that incredible speed for which the species is known, flashed in again, and this time when the starlings flushed, he nailed one in mid air. I watched him tear apart the starling for breakfast, then I returned to looking for deer. The goshawk must have seen the whites of my eyes and figured they looked small and edible. All of a sudden, it was right in my face. I jerked my head away from the hawk's talons as fast as I could and slammed the back of my head hard into that solid oak tree. I was wearing a safety harness, which was good, because I saw stars and heard that funny music you hear when it's almost lights out.

The strangest encounter I've had with a raptor was in northern Saskatchewan. It was very cold, something like 25-below zero, and I was sitting in an open treestand slowly freezing to death and questioning whether even one of the province's big bucks was worth the torture. You don't see much wildlife that far north in winter, so when a great gray owl glided through the woods and landed on a burnt snag 30 yards away, I was delighted for the company and spent the next few minutes studying the giant bird through my binoculars. The owl must have seen me move and launched itself off that charred snag and headed in my direction.

Being a veteran of several encounters with hawks and owls, I put my arm over my face to protect myself, but I need not have worried, because the owl meant me no harm. I'm sure that the owl had probably never seen a human being before, and it was just curious about that blob in the tree. It landed on a branch jutting out an angle just above my right shoulder.

There the owl perched, maybe six feet away from my head, looking me over closely with those large, wondering owl eyes. The great gray is a big bird, standing 30 inches or better, and at first, it was a bit unnerving. But the longer the owl sat there staring at me, the more comfortable I grew to his presence.

I don't really believe in reincarnation — where we come back to earth as some other critter after we die — but I got to thinking, looking into that big, round face that the owl certainly did bear a strong resemblance to my Grandpa Henry. I started calling the owl "Hank," and we carried on quite a one-sided, whispered conversation for nearly a half hour before the owl tired of my reminiscing and, without so much as a hoot good-bye, just glided off on those incredibly silent wings that owls possess.

Some nonhunters think that hunting is mostly about killing, but it is not, and these encounters underscore that for me. For the life of me, I cannot remember if I shot anything on any of these days, but I've never forgotten the details of each encounter with these majestic birds of prey.

The second-chance buck

On New Year's Day 1999, a blizzard that would eventually dump a foot of snow and send temperatures into that 20-below range every night for the next week, swept across southern Iowa. Nearly everyone in the community of Centerville, Iowa, was snug at home watching New Year's parades and bowl games. But not the "Maddy Boys."

Like every other year, Jason, Keenan, and Stan Maddy take advantage of Christmas vacation when the schools are closed for the holidays. Stan's a teacher, and when school is closed and deer season is open, that's where you'll find Stan and his boys.

The plan that morning was simple. Stan would take a stand at a major crossing on a particularly steep-sided, oak-studded ridge. Jason and Keenan would slowly work their way through the timber toward Stan — call it a still-hunt, driving, stand-hunting combination.

An hour passed, and

Centerville, Iowa resident Stan Maddy took advantage of a second chance at this buck, which he killed via muzzleloader.

Stan huddled deeper into his heavy coat against the fierce winds driving the snow like shotgun pellets. Then he spotted a doe slipping up the sidehill toward his position. A big buck followed. When the two deer reached the top of the ridge and the buck stepped into the open, Stan lined up the crosshairs of his scope (you can use scopes during the Iowa muzzleloader season) high on the buck's back and touched the trigger of his .50 caliber.

Through the smoke, Stan saw the big buck drop in its tracks, but the buck quickly was back on his feet and running through the snow. When the boys arrived, all three hunters took the track. There was little blood, but through well-honed tracking skills they stayed on the buck's trail as it plowed on through the building snow.

Finally the buck crossed an open area where the drifting snow had obliterated any sign. A long-faced group of hunters drove home that evening.

I heard the story of the big buck from Stan and the boys when we met at Bratz's Texaco before dawn the next morning. The Maddy Boys and I have become good friends, and we hunt together when I'm in their neck of the woods. We made a couple of pushes through the deep snow that morning, then Stan and his sons went back to look for the big buck some more. I offered to go along, but Stan said that finding the big buck now was a real long-shot. He had to look, but suggested that I get on stand for the evening. He was right; they never found the big buck.

Now flash ahead a year. The Iowa muzzleloader season is once again in full swing. School is out for the Christmas holidays, and Stan and his sons are deer hunting.

They're back in the timber where Stan had hit the big buck the previous year, and he's sitting on the same ridge. The boys are still-hunting through the timber in Stan's direction. Stan tries to stay alert, to keep his mind in the game, but his thoughts wander to the events of a year ago.

"I know what I did wrong," Stan told me once. "I over-estimated the range. Maybe it was the driving snow or maybe I was just so excited that I thought the buck was farther away than he was. Whatever the case, I held high on the buck's back thinking that the buck was just over 100 yards away, and with my rifle sighted in at 100 yards, my bullet would drop a couple inches at that range. Later I stepped it off. The buck was only 70 yards away. I probably hit him right where I was aiming."

On stand, while playing the events of the previous year over in his mind, he hears a noise behind him. Deer move toward him, and one of them is a buck, a big buck! This time, when the buck is in range, Stan puts the crosshairs on the buck's chest and squeezes the trigger. When Jason and Kennan arrive on the scene, jubilation ensues on the ridge, complete with high-fives, back-slapping, and picture-taking. This is a family affair, and the whole gang shares in the moment.

"The buck looked an awful lot like the one from the year before," Stan told me, "but I didn't even dare get my hopes up that it could be him. I mean, what are the odds?"

But when Stan and the boys began caping the deer out for the trip to the taxidermist, there was the proof. The wound was nicely healed. Stan had hit the buck right where he had held the crosshairs that day in the blizzard, high on the back. The big slug had passed just above the buck's spine, close enough for the shock to drop the buck momentarily, but not close enough to keep him down. Bleeding from such a wound is minimal, which explains the skimpy blood trail they had followed that day in the blizzard.

Life is full of second chances. I'm mighty glad that my friend Stan got his.

Half a trophy

On the last day of the year 2000, I pointed my well-traveled pickup south and made the 325-mile drive to my friend Tony Knight's place just west of Centerville, Iowa.

Tony and his wife, Rose, let me bunk in their pole shed when I'm hunting their neck of the woods, but it's not as bad as it sounds since the rear third of the shed has been partitioned off into living quarters complete with bunks, stove, 'frig and even a TV. Rose usually feels sorry for me having to eat my own cooking, so she always invites me in for supper.

The living was easy, but the hunting was tough.

Actually, I thought it might be fairly easy to hang my tag on a good buck that season. We'd had the snow and cold, which is exactly what I wish for when hunting late-season whitetails. The combination of snow and cold forces deer to concentrate on remaining food sources, and that provides a pattern.

But this year, things just did not work out that way. Tony wisely asked me not to hunt his farm because he, his son, Billy, and a couple of friends already had taken four dandy bucks.

Even though I had the assistance of the "Maddy Boys," Stan, Keane and Jason, and my old friend Bruce Watley, I just could not get on a buck. In fact, after hunting a solid week, I had yet to lay eyes on a buck. So I drove home and spent a couple of days catching up on business in the office.

I considered calling it quits. The weather had warmed, and my chances of seeing a good buck were slim. Indeed, they were getting slimmer with each passing day, since a good number of the bucks already had shed their antlers and more were dropping every day. But persistence pays, so on Monday, Jan. 8, with only a couple of days to hunt before the season ended (on Jan. 10), I threw my sleeping bag, muzzle-loader, and some grub in the pickup and headed south.

The first evening was a bust — not a single deer. The next morning was a repeat performance, and I was beginning to think I did not know much about white-tailed deer. But I believe in sticking with it and hunting hard and smart until the final bell, so that afternoon found me prowling the hard-wood ridges. A well-trafficked trail appeared about mid-afternoon, and I settled over it for what I expected would be another long, cold vigil.

A stray hound made short work of this stand site. I heard it barking down in the valley, and pretty soon a group of five does came hurrying down the trail. They had just disap-peared into the timber when a big-bodied deer broke across the ridge, then stopped 50 yards in front of me to look back in the direction from which it had come.

Just by the shape of the deer's body and his square head, I figured I was look-ing at a buck that had shed his antlers. My binocu-lars confirmed my suspicions. The barking grew loud-er and two more bucks joined the antlerless buck. One was an 8-point, the other a 10-point. Both were 2½-year-old bucks.

With all of the hound activity in that valley, I decid-ed to move out and backtrack to anoth-er valley. Normally, I love to still-hunt, but the warm spell had left the snow crusted and noisy,

The author's initial disappointment at shooting a one-antlered buck gave way to the satisfaction that always comes with successfully hunting a mature whitetail.

and even with a fairly stiff wind blowing, there was no way I could slip up on a deer without it hearing me first. But out of habit, when I came to the crest of a ridge, I just naturally slowed down and snuck slowly over the lip. The buck below me must have been pawing through the crusted snow for acorns and making so much noise in the process that he didn't hear me.

There was nothing wrong with his eyes. When I popped into view, he blew out of there at full speed, raced down the side of the hill, crossed a deep ditch, and started up the far side. I grabbed the dog whistle I wear around my neck just for such occasions and gave a loud, sharp blast on the whistle. Usually, a deer will stop when it hears the whistle. This one skidded to a stop right behind a clump of trees. I could see his butt sticking out one side and his head from the eye forward sticking out the other.

Through my binoculars I could see a long main beam jutting out toward the end of his nose, a sure sign of a mature buck. I knew he would not stand still for more than a few seconds and when he departed, it would likely be at full tilt. There were a lot of tree limbs between me and the buck, but with the 2X6 scope cranked up to maximum magnification, I found a small opening in front of the buck.

I put the crosshairs in front of his black nose and a nanosecond later when the buck bolted, I hit the trigger. I was shooting a Knight Super DISC .45 muzzleloaders and feeding it a 165-grain Barnes saboted bullet pushed along by 150 grains of Pyrodex. This is the flattest shooting frontloader I've ever stoked, and that flat trajectory was key for making the shot. The buck died instantly with a broken neck.

Seventy-five yards from the buck, I knew something was not right. His head was lying too flat. My trophy only had one antler. Judging by the freshness of the blood on the buck's forehead, he had probably shed the other antler that day. I spent a half hour searching the sidehill and retracing his route in case the antler had dropped during his escape, but no luck.

As you can see in the photo on Page 117, the buck is a mature animal, probably 3½ years old. The single antler scores 66 inches, which means that if the other antler matches and given an 18-inch spread, the buck would gross around 152.

At first, I was disappointed. I felt cheated. Had I known the buck only had one side, I would not have pulled the trigger. But on the long drive home, I realized that one antler or two, the buck was still a mature whitetail. He still possessed the same uncanny sense of smell, the keen ears, and the good eyes. He was still the same magician at appearing and disappearing, something his kind does better than any other big game animal.

And for my part, I'd hunted him as well and as hard as I knew how, and in the end, the gods of the hunt had smiled on me once again.

So if one day you should visit my cluttered office, you'll notice that on the wall, surrounded by more perfect specimens, is the mount of a one-antlered buck. Go ahead and snicker, it won't bother me, because that half-rack is a trophy in every respect.

Mutt, Jeff and a horse named Cowboy

One of my more interesting whitetail hunts of 1999 took place in southwest Kansas in late September. Kansas is one of a handful of states and provinces that offers muzzleloaders a crack at whitetails before the firearms season.

Because I had also drawn an archery elk tag for the Gila Wilderness in New Mexico, by the time I got out of the mountains and drove to Kansas, there were only four days left in the Kansas muzzleloader season when I pulled into the yard of Jeff and Teresa Louderback. After introductions I was ushered to "my" room. By the time I had showered and changed into hunting clothes, Mike Mitchell, Jeff's friend and partner, had arrived.

They were quite a pair. Jeff is a cowboy, born and bred. His family had ranched the land for generations. He's lean, wiry, rawhide tough, walks with a hitch in his gait that suggests he may have been thrown off a few rodeo broncs, and like most cowboys, chooses his words carefully. Mike is about twice the size of Jeff and as out-going and gregarious as Jeff is quiet. I nicknamed the transplanted Vermonter "Mutt" and from then on the two would be Mutt and Jeff. Both, like me, love to hunt for mature whitetail bucks. We hit it off quickly.

After an uneventful first-morning hunt, Mutt and Jeff put on a little drive. I slipped into position just across an old fenceline and waited. It wasn't long before I heard the unmistakable sound of something with hooves hurrying in my direction. By the sounds of it, this had to be one of the big bucks Mutt and Jeff had told me bedded in this patch of timber. I slid the muzzleloader over the deadfall before me and got ready. But what broke out of the timber and jumped the fence was not a big buck, but a long-legged, camel-necked cow elk! Here I was — fresh off a bust of an elk hunt — and right in front of me stood 500 pounds of the best-eating meat in the world — in Kansas of all places! Turns out the cow was the last survivor of a herd of nine that had worn out its welcome with area ranchers and

MUTT, JEFF AND A HORSE NAMED COWBOY

farmers. When Mutt and Jeff arrived on the scene I told them that they were accomplished "elk drivers," but they needed a little more practice in the deer department.

Each morning and evening, I continued to see deer off stand, but the big boys were playing hard to get. On the last morning of my hunt, Jeff dropped me off in the river bottom timber before first light. My plan was to slowly still-hunt through the timber until mid-morning, when Mutt or Jeff would pick me up a mile west of my starting point.

I love this style of hunting, but I didn't get very far. Shortly after full light, I caught movement in the timber ahead of me. The binoculars revealed a doe and fawn working in my direction. I stepped behind the trunk of a tremendous cottonwood tree and waited. I didn't know it then, but I would end up standing behind that tree trunk for two hours.

As I watched the doe and fawn slowly amble through the timber, one or the other would stop frequently to browse or graze. Then I detected more movement farther down the river. More deer were making their way back from the alfalfa fields where they had fed during the night. Early in the season, it's not unusual to find bucks still in bachelor groups, and this gang had five members. All of them were one-year-old bucks — the biggest a basket-rack 8-point. Within minutes another doe, this one with twin fawns, appeared, then two bucks and a doe. These two bucks were both dandies; one a narrow, heavy-antlered 10-point, the other a high-racked 8-point with thinner tines.

A combination cattle and deer drive featuring Jeff Louderback and "Cowboy the horse" helped produce a successful Kansas hunt for the author.

All of this makes it sound like I was hunting a deer farm, but I wasn't. By dumb luck I'd stumbled into the area the deer intended to bed, and now all I could do was stand behind that cottonwood and play my hand.

Speaking of playing, that's exactly what the deer commenced. With the exception of the first doe and fawn, which nipped dried leaves from a clump of buck brush — a low-growing shrub common in Western states — all of the deer were gathered in the grassy bed of the dried-up river about 200 yards from where I stood. The bucks would lower their heads and spar, while the fawns chased each other across the river bed at full speed.

White-tailed deer are social creatures, and I've seen this playful behavior demonstrated many times. It went on for a half hour, and then the big boy arrived on the scene. When he did, every deer turned its attention toward him. So did I.

He was a 9-point, but what a 9-point! Given the sag to his belly and the sway in his back, this buck was an old-timer. It was interesting to watch the other deer interact with him. The does ignored him, but each of the seven other bucks took turns approaching the big buck for a little touch of the horns. Nothing violent. You couldn't even call it sparring really, just a white-tailed version of a human handshake, I suspect.

I dug out my grunt call and gave a couple of contact grunts. The old boy stared in my direction, and then started walking toward me. He had covered maybe 50 yards and was still coming when one of the young bucks dashed over to him, put his head down and greeted the old buck with lowered antlers. The big buck forgot all about the grunt that had attracted him and obliged the youngster with a little playful head-shaking. Then he turned around and walked away.

I tried a few more grunts, but it was obvious the buck had lost interest, so I tucked the call away. With my luck, I figured I'd accidentally call in one of the small bucks and blow the whole deal.

In the next 10 minutes all of the deer bedded. The doe and fawn lay down in the buck brush clump where they'd been feeding, and the five young bucks chose a house-sized thicket not far away from them. The two bigger bucks and the doe bedded 60 yards in front of me, and the big boy went off by himself in the opposite direction. I had a good idea where he bedded because I had jumped a big deer there two mornings earlier.

For another hour, I stood behind the cottonwood tree. When deer first bed down, they spend an hour or so relaxing and chewing their cud. They keep their heads erect during this time and though not on full alert, they still know what's happening around them. If I tried to slip away early, I'd risk spooking the bedded deer, so I just stood in the warming morning sun and watched the racks of the two larger bucks above the dry grass.

When both racks disappeared, I knew that the bucks were dozing off, so I dropped to my belly and crawled the 20 yards to the steep bank of the dry river bed and slithered down the bank. Once in the river bed, I used the steep sides to hide from the deer and hurried off. Mike and Jeff were a mile upriver waiting where they had expected me to exit. I circled wide of the area where the deer were bedded and hoofed it over to the guys. On the ride back to the ranch I filled them in on the morning.

While I wolfed down some breakfast, Jeff called his dad, Larry, to see if he could help drive that patch of timber the big buck had entered. As luck would have it, Larry and Jeff's uncle, Max, who also ranches in the area, had just loaded horses into the trailer and was preparing to round up some cattle in the same stretch of river bottom.

By the time I'd filled my empty tank, we had plans for a deer/cattle drive. Jeff, Larry, and Max rode their horses through the rangeland to the far end of the timber, while Mike dropped me off a quarter mile from where I'd spent the morning watching the deer. I made my way back up the dried river bed to within 100 yards of where the two bucks and the doe were bedded, slithered back up the steep bank, and took up my position behind a bleached deadfall where I had a good field of fire for 100 yards in all directions, as well as a good view up the river. Mike, who also had a tag, would cover a brushy finger exiting the timber. Experience had taught him that deer sometimes cut out across the open pasture land.

Since the cattle/deer drive was approaching from the direction where the big buck had bedded, and since he was the most distant of the deer congregating in the river bed that morning, I expected (and hoped) that he would be the first deer I'd see, but that's not how it shook out.

An hour passed before anything happened. I could not yet hear the approaching horsemen and the cattle ahead of them, but the deer could. A doe and two fawns filed past. Then the five young bucks were on their feet, all five staring in the direction of the approaching cattle drive. About the time they broke and trotted down the trail 10 yards from me, I began to faintly hear the complaining bellows of the cows. The doe and her fawn rose from the buck brush and melted away, but still no sign of the big buck.

Then the two larger bucks and the doe stood and stared in the direction of the approaching cattle for a minute or two. Evidently deciding the cows would not pass around them, they hurried in my direction. The trio passed 20 yards in front of me, crossed the dry river bed and stopped on the opposite bank to stare back over their haunches.

Both bucks were very tempting, and I had a bad feeling in my gut. The drive already had passed where I expected the big 9-point had bedded, and it was the last day of my hunt. But. Always but. No, I had come to Kansas for a crack at a giant deer for which this state is famous, and I knew that such a deer had been oh so close just hours earlier. I believed that he was still in the timber, which right now was filled with the "hee-ahh cows" of the cowboys, the creak of leather, the jingle of bits and bridles, and the incessant complaints of the cows and calves.

No, I would wait and... just then, a brown streak went sneaking through the bleached grass growing in the dried river bed 400 yards away and well behind the advancing deer/cattle drive. Before I put my binoculars to my eyes I knew it was him. The old veteran had held tight and let the cows and the calves and the horses and riders pass him, probably within yards, maybe feet. Nerves of titanium.

Just that quickly I elected to take the heavy-horned 10-pointer still standing with his buddy and the doe 60 yards away on the opposite bank of the river. Just as quickly the trio decided the cows were close enough and they broke. I swung the heavy 26-inch barrel of the Knight DISC rifle ahead of the surging buck and slapped the trigger as the glow of the fiber-optic sights passed the buck's nose. The 250-grain Barnes bullet got to the deer quicker than I had anticipated, catching the buck in the neck, putting the 200-pound, grain-fattened Kansas whitetail down in mid-stride.

When I walked over to the fallen buck, I was in for two more surprises. For one thing, the buck was bigger than I had thought. Usually, on the ground, it's the other way around. The other surprise was that lying alongside the fallen buck's broken neck was a small four-point shed. I picked it up and had my taxidermist incorporate it into the mount of the Kansas buck.

After congratulations all around, Max and Larry kept the cattle moving while Jeff threw a rope around the buck's antlers, tied it around the saddle horn, and touched his spurs lightly to his horse Cowboy's flanks. It was my easiest deer drag ever!

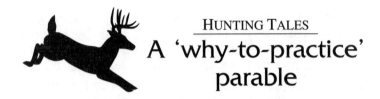

A 'why-to-practice' parable

On a hunt for white-tailed deer in Canada a few years back I was fortunate enough to take a nice buck on the fourth day of a six-day hunt. Since I'm not much on just lying around camp and vegetating, I anxiously accepted an invitation from a middle-aged hunter from Pennsylvania to accompany him on his hunt. There was plenty of room for both of us in the ground blind, and he assured me that he would welcome my company.

The next morning found us slipping into the ground blind just before dawn. I fussed around in one corner getting my stool and seat cushion set up and laying out my camera gear, while "Joe" — as we will call him — settled into his corner. It was a cold, still morning, about minus 10, and the branches of the naked popple trees around our stand suspended motionless.

When it grew lighter, I could tell the sky was overcast, which meant the day would remain cold. That was bad for us, but good for hunting. Deer in Canada move much better during cold weather.

Joe was bundled up in everything he owned, and being short in stature and a bit on the thick side, he reminded me of the Pillsbury Doughboy. Despite his layers of clothing and the Mickey Mouse boots, he was still cold. I sat comfortable and cozy in my Heater Body Suit, and after about an hour Joe whispered to me that he was going to get him one of them "body bags" when he got back home.

Joe was pouring a cup of coffee with his umpteenth donut, when I spotted our first deer of the morning slipping through the bush. My binoculars confirmed that the deer was a doe, but with the rut just winding down I watched behind the doe, and sure enough — within a few seconds here came one of those 300-pound-plus brutes for which the provinces of western Canada are famous.

I whispered to Joe that a big buck was about to step into the cut-line about 100 yards in front of our stand. Joe spilled his coffee, choked on a mouthful of donut, fumbled around trying to remove his mittens, and snatched his rifle from where it had been leaning against the corner of the plywood blind. The buck was now nose-to-tail with the doe standing broadside just shy of 100 yards down the cut-line. A chip-shot.

As Joe settled into the stock I put my fingers to my ears and waited for the blast. But instead of a KABOOM all I heard was a dull, metallic click and Joe saying "Oh #@#@."

Joe had forgotten to chamber a round after we had entered the blind that morning. He reacted — a flinch of monumental proportions — as if the rifle had fired.

Luckily for Joe, our plywood box deadened some of the sound, because it took some fumbling before Joe had finally managed to chamber a round. The buck was still intent on the apathetic doe who ignored old lover boy. Once again Joe settled into the stock and I put my fingers to my ears. This time the .300 Weatherby Magnum bellowed when Joe jerked that trigger. But instead of falling over, the buck just jerked his head up, and he and the doe looked around for the source of the sudden noise. Joe sat there.

"You missed," I hissed. "Jack in another one."

This jolted Joe into action and he frantically worked the bolt to chamber a fresh round, but in his haste he short-stroked the bolt and ended up with the fishing equivalent of a backlash, as a new round attempted to feed into the chamber while the empty was still stuck in the extractor. Joe fumbled to clear the jam, the doe decided to move on, and with a flick of her tail, disappeared into the timber. The buck followed.

When the deer left, I looked over at Joe. He was still clearing the jam in his rifle and blood was dripping all over his ample belly from a nasty gash above his right eyebrow where the scope had cut him.

It probably wasn't all that funny, but it took all my will-power to keep from laughing.

What's this little episode have to do with you? I happen to live just a few miles from the Byron Sportsman's Club rifle range, and on a calm day or when the wind is out of the north, I can hear the reports of high-powered rifles or shotguns being fired. The week before the firearms deer season opens, it is a steady barrage, but other than that, I rarely hear any shooting other than the Thursday evening sporting clays shoot.

Most of the Joes of the world dig out their deer rifle, muzzle-loader, or slug gun the week before the season. Odds are it's the first time they've had the gun in their hands since last season. When they get to the range, they put up a target, nestle the rifle into sandbags, get comfortable at the bench, and squeeze off a few rounds to make sure that Old Betsy is "still dead-on." They call it practice. That's like calling a hot air balloon ride a space shuttle launch.

Start practicing early. When I practice, I sit at the bench only long enough to ensure that the rifle and scope have done their job. I've never sat in a stand that affords me a bench seat and sandbag rest. Maybe that's why five-shot groups you can cover with a quarter have never impressed me much.

The real fun begins after you've sighted in the rifle, muzzle-loader, or slug gun. That's when I get off the bench and shoot while sitting on my butt on the ground, kneeling, and even off-hand, although I cannot recall the last critter I've shot from the incredibly unstable off-hand position. Each time I fire a shot, I work the bolt quickly and smoothly and chamber a fresh round, so that when I get to the woods, the motion is automatic.

When I sight in, I like to use those nifty yellow and black Shoot-N-C targets that allow you to quickly and easily see where the bullets strike. They eliminate all of that walking back and forth to the target or peering through a spotting scope. (By the way, kids get a big kick out of seeing the yellow splash when shooting .22s at these targets, which keeps them interested in shooting longer).

When the real practice begins, I use cardboard cut-outs in the shape of a deer. I've yet to see a deer in the woods with a big bull's-eye behind his shoulder. Using the cardboard silhouettes trains my eye to find the best place to put the bullet.

When hunting, I use the best ammunition, and my rifle, shot-gun, or muzzleloader is sighted in with that preferred ammo. But I'm not about to shoot up a box or two of premium ammo during my practice sessions. When practicing I use less expensive ammunition. Often I put a box or two of ammo through my .22 rifle first, then switch over to the deer gun. My cardboard deer target doesn't care.

Time constraints are no excuse for being unfamiliar with your gun. Take the time to remove your rifle from storage each evening, and practice slipping the safety off quietly. Look through the scope or line up the iron sights on that nail hole in the wall. Do it several times, shoulder the stock, and line up the sights or crosshairs. Practice doing it with your eyes closed.

Before long, you'll be lined up on that nail hole each time you open your eyes. If you shoot a pump, lever-action, or bolt-action, work that action so that when the time comes in the woods when you need a quick second shot you won't fumble around. Dry-fire until you're confident that you're not jerking on the trigger.

Practice, and your deer gun will be as comfortable as an old friend on opening day, instead of a clumsy stranger.

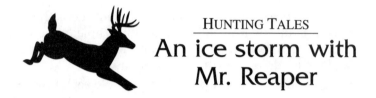

An ice storm with Mr. Reaper

Many readers remember that on Halloween Day 1991, the damnedest ice storm the north country has ever seen swept across Minnesota and northern Iowa. The storm spared the Twin Cities and the central regions the ice, but well over a foot of snow still fell. As freakish as that much snow is in October, it was the ice that was unbelievable. It built up so heavy on powerlines that those big erector set things that hold up the wires crumpled under the weight, and much of the region was without power for a week or more. Giant maples, towering cottonwoods, and monster white oaks that had stood for 100 years against everything nature could dish out, toppled by the thousands in that storm. I know. I watched a bunch of them crash from my front-row seat in a treestand 20 feet off the ground on an oak-studded ridge not far from Lanesboro.

Oh, I knew I should have climbed down when the rain began to freeze to everything about mid-afternoon, but I didn't. After all, it was Halloween. Forget ghosts and goblins, and trick or treat; Halloween is prime time for an all-day stint on stand. Bucks get rammy by Halloween. They're ready to breed big-time, but the does aren't ready, so the bucks wander around making scrapes, destroying little saplings, and duking it out with each other while pestering the poor does. It's a heady time for the bowhunter; we wait all year for it.

So against my better judgement, I remained and watched the ice coat every branch, every bush, and every stubborn leaf clinging to the red oaks dotting the ridge. Within just a few minutes, pencil-thin twigs transformed into finger-thick icicles. Then the wind started to blow, and I remember thinking that the woods sounded like a giant crystal chandelier.

Like many bowhunters, when I settle into my stand, I take an extra arrow and lay it across a nearby branch, so that if I miss, I can quickly grab the arrow and release a second shot. But today, the wind dislodged my arrow and it fell.

No big deal; it's happened many times. The broadhead is the heaviest component of the arrow, so it always lands point down. But this time the arrow glanced off a branch just before it would have landed broadhead down, did a nifty flip, and landed broadhead up right at the base of the tree where I perched. Call it a one-stick punji pit.

I would have climbed down, I swear, but you see, the deer were going nuts. White-tailed deer have an excellent internal weather-forecast system, and they knew that this storm would force them to bed for a day or two, so they were out in force. There were does, fawns, and small bucks all over.

Still, I should have climbed down, but I could not get the image of that 10-point out of my head. I'd missed the big buck on opening day just a couple hundred yards from my stand. I had not seen him since, but I'd seen his track a few times, so I knew he was still around. On a day like this, even a mature buck would be on his feet and moving, so I sat.

The big buck came all right, but when he did, the woods was a nightmare of wind-whipped, slamming, ice-caked branches as the northwest wind increased in intensity. He came from behind and to my right, walking head down into the brunt of the storm. Being right-handed, I had to stand to shoot. My stand platform, like everything else was caked with an inch or more of ice.

When I stood and turned to get in position, even though I moved as cautiously as possible, my feet went out from under me. The safety belt abruptly halted my rapid descent, but the sudden cinching of the strap around my chest knocked the wind out of me like a nasty right uppercut to the mid-section. The buck — only 10 yards away — never even looked up. I tried to draw on him as I hung by the belt, but my arrow had been dislodged in the fall. I watched him walk away.

"That's it," I remember thinking to myself. "I'm going to get my stuff and get the hell out of here. This is crazy."

But it wasn't quite that easy. I couldn't get back into the stand. The stand and the tree were all sheathed in ice. Try as I might, I couldn't get a grip on anything to hoist my 200 pounds aboard. After 10 minutes, I was exhausted from the effort and decided that the best thing I could do was hug the trunk, cut the safety belt, and slide down to the first big branch, which was about five feet below my feet.

Problem was, my knife remained in my fanny pack hanging from a branch stub above my stand, and my quiver, full of arrows with sharp broadheads, was hanging near the fanny pack. I was in trouble, and for the first time since 'Nam, that once all-too-familiar copper-like taste of fear coated my tongue.

Maybe fear provided the adrenaline rush I needed to pull myself back aboard the stand. I don't know how, but I finally made it. I rested a few minutes, undid the safety belt, and started descending.

The metal screw-in tree steps were like popsicles. I moved as slowly and carefully as I could, but when my foot slipped off one of the steps about 12 feet above the ground, I began to fall. It only takes a nano-second for a 200-pound Irishman to drop a dozen feet, but it was enough time for me to remember that broadhead sticking straight up along the base of the tree.

I tried to push off the tree, but there was not time. I landed on the small of my back against the side of that oak, and I just knew the arrow had run clean through me. There was no pain, but big wounds, I knew from past experience, take a while before they hurt. How many times had I zipped an arrow through a deer and watched them casually walk off, only to fall over dead within steps?

I lay there, the freezing rain pelting my bare face, waiting for the warm ooze of blood. If the broadhead was through me, my odds of making it the half mile back to my pickup were not good. Finally I checked things out. Carefully, I reached across my body with my left hand and felt gingerly for the broadhead. When I felt the sharp blades, I ran my bare fingers down the shaft. Yes, it was through my coat. I could hardly bring myself to look at my fingers.

"Funny thing" I thought to myself, "all of these years, when I run my fingers down an arrow shaft, I'm hoping to see blood, but now…." When I finally looked, my fingers were clean, no blood! I pulled the arrow through my coat.

Later that evening, when I finally returned to the little trailer on the banks of Duschee Creek and built a fire in the old wood stove, I found that the broadhead had sliced through not only my jacket, but the wool sweater I wore beneath the jacket as well.

Though I never saw that buck again, I learned several lessons that afternoon:

1. No matter how hard-core you might be, there are weather conditions when hunting is not safe;

2. Throw away all of your safety belts and get a good shoulder harness;

3. Always carry a knife in your pocket or on your belt, just in case;

4. Don't lay that extra arrow on a branch, use a screw-in arrow-holder instead;

5. Don't laugh at guys who carry a cell phone into the woods.

The Velvet Buck

W hen most hunters think of Montana, they think of bugling bull elk, or maybe wide-racked mule deer. But it's the white-tailed deer, my favorite big game species, which has most often drawn me to Montana. In 2001, I made my third trip to Montana's Milk River country in search of one of the big, grain-fattened whitetails that call this strip of extreme northern Montana home.

The Milk River twists and turns its way through hundreds of thousands of acres of pasture, wheat stubble, and alfalfa fields. The deer feed in the alfalfa and bed in the cottonwoods and willows along the river.

The deer here are relatively simple to pattern. Often, we sit on the high bluffs overlooking the green fields and river bottom and glass in the mornings or evening. It's easy to see which fields the deer, especially big bucks, are using most. But that's where the easy part ends. Although the big bucks here are more visible than in most places you'll encounter whitetails, a mature buck is a mature buck no matter the habitat it calls home. Taking one, especially with bow and arrow, requires hard work, patience, and a dose of good fortune.

It was the fifth day of our hunt before John Dudley, from Sparta, Wis., dropped the string on a dandy, 135-inch, 8-point buck to break the ice. John and Don Kisky, who hail from southern Iowa, had to leave the next morning, but Bill Jordan, the man who brought you Realtree camo, and I decided to extend our stay and work overtime for the big bucks.

Don had been hunting a big buck that we had named "The Velvet Buck" because he was the only buck we saw with his antlers still sheathed in soft velvet. The Velvet Buck had a way of staying one step ahead of Don and his cameraman, Glenn Garner, both of whom are excellent deer hunters.

If the buck came out under a certain cottonwood one

evening, Don and Glenn would hang a stand in that cottonwood for the next evening's hunt. Guess where the buck
would walk? You guessed it, right under the stand they had
hunted the evening before. Don and Glenn even took to using
a flat-bottomed boat in the mornings to allow them to slip in
the backside of the cover where the buck was bedding. They
saw the Velvet Buck each morning and evening they hunted,
but when the hunt was over for Don and Glenn, Old Velvet
was still roaming.

Bill really wanted to hunt the Velvet Buck on film, knowing
that it would make for a unique hunt. He asked if I would like
to have a go at the deer, and I jumped at the chance, because
I've never had the opportunity to hunt a deer in velvet. By
now we were all convinced that the Velvet Buck was one of
those unique deer, which for whatever reason, was not going
to shed its velvet. The only way to discover the reason would
be to put the buck on the ground.

The next morning,
Bill, his cameraman,
Nick Mundt, my
cameraman, Mark
Womack, and I
maneuvered a cou-
ple of big round
bales into position
for a ground blind in
the field the Velvet
Buck had been visit-
ing each evening. I
would hunt from the
hay bale blind while
Mark captured the
action for Realtree
Outdoors television
and Monster Bucks
video from his perch
in a treestand high
behind the hay
bales. I've hunted
from hay bale blinds
before and have
found them to be

A hay bale set up in Montana put the author in
position to take the Velvet Buck in October, 2001.

very effective. In a field where round bales are scattered about, deer don't seem to notice if you move a couple to make a blind.

That afternoon, Donna Korman, the best darn cook in all of Montana, dropped Mark and I off at the field where we'd spend the next few hours. Mark and I were both dressed in Scent-Lok suits, and as an added precaution we sprayed each other down with some scent-killing spray. With the number of deer visiting the field, I knew that we would both have to fool the noses of a lot of deer if the Velvet Buck was to appear.

It was a warm, sun-drenched afternoon, and it seemed like an eternity before the first does and fawns filtered into the field and made their way slowly toward my blind. I held my breath. If the does smelled me or became suspicious of my blind, the bucks would not follow. Ten minutes later with the does and fawns feeding all around me, some within just a few yards, I allowed myself to relax a bit. It looked like the precautions to control our odor were paying off. If the Velvet Buck followed his pattern, the plan would work.

The bachelor groups of bucks were just starting to break up, but I knew the Velvet Buck was still hanging out with a couple of young 10-point bucks and a heavy, mature 9-point. When those three bucks arrived on the scene and began munching alfalfa in front of my blind, I grabbed my bow. But the Velvet Buck did not show.

The other three bucks continued to feed around my blind, and at one point the 9-pointer strolled over to the hay bale blind where I crouched and actually grabbed a mouthful of hay from one of the bales. He was so close that I could hear him chewing!

And then, with the sun sinking, the Velvet Buck strode onto the scene.

The only problem now was that his buddy, the 9-point was standing 20 feet in front of me and facing my direction. There was no way I could draw without him spotting the movement, so I crouched in the blind clutching my bow and worked my only option: I waited.

Finally, when the Velvet Buck was nearly out of my effective range, the 9-pointer turned his head. I took a quick reading with my rangefinder, drew, settled the pin, and sent the arrow flashing across the Montana dusk.

The Velvet Buck was dead in seconds, and Mark captured the whole incredible hunt on film.

What a way to start the 2001 season!

One spooky Halloween buck

A deer stand might be nothing more than the broad beam of a stout oak to lean your back against when you plant your butt on the ground. Or it might be a portable tree-stand, or a permanent stand constructed on private land. These are all common deer stands. But while digging through my slide files looking for pictures to illustrate a magazine article one day, I came across a couple of photos that reminded me of a few of the rather strange stands I've sat in over the years.

Once, while hunting the late muzzleloader season in southern Iowa, I found an out-of-the-way harvested cornfield tucked back into a little valley.

A quick inspection for tracks and droppings showed that deer were visiting the picked cornfield on a regular basis. Heavy timber bordered the cornfield on three sides. On the fourth side was a deep ditch grown up to scrub brush and small trees. These ditches, caused by erosion, are common in

Old farm equipment, and on occasion, abandoned houses like this old Colorado homestead, have served the author well as makeshift deer hunting stand sites.

southern Iowa and northern Missouri. A generation or two of farmers had been discarding old machinery in that ditch. The grain hopper of a John Deere combine became my stand the next day. It was pretty comfortable, and the rim of the hopper provided a nice rest for my muzzleloader.

As the wind picked up ahead of an approaching storm, I was glad for the protection the steel walls of the hopper provided. A pair of field mice, cute little buggers with white feet and long whiskers, had a nest somewhere in that hulk of a rusted combine. Their route to the outside world was up through the hole in the bottom of the grain hopper. Then, without effort, they would scamper up the steel walls and disappear over the edge.

Sometimes in minutes, sometimes longer, they would tip back over the edge, this time with their little cheeks crammed with seeds for their winter cache. At first they were leery of me, but when they discovered that the big orange blob in the hopper meant them no harm, they pretty much accepted me as just another old, rusty piece of machinery (which is becoming a more accurate description of me with each passing year.)

By the end of the day the mice figured it was easier to scamper up my leg and over my shoulder to exit the hopper than to scale the rusted, steel walls. I thought to myself that neither my wife nor my three daughters would find the antics of the mice quite as entertaining as I did.

In case you're wondering, no, I never did shoot a deer from that combine hopper. I sat in it all day because, like I mentioned, there was a winter storm brewing, and I figured deer would be tanking up prior to the storm. My journal indicates that I saw 23 deer that day, but none of them were the caliber of buck I sought. I'm real fussy when hunting places with the trophy potential of southern Iowa.

Years before, however, I killed a little buck with my bow while perched on another old combine in an abandoned grove in southern Minnesota.

Once during a hard, cold November rain, I huddled for several hours in what had once been the root cellar of one of the many long abandoned homesteads dotting the Whitewater Wildlife Management Area. It had been dug into the sidehill and lined on the floor, and part way up the walls with slabs of limestone. It smelled like old earth, and I kept thinking that the old root cellar would make a nifty rattlesnake den!

The spookiest stand I've ever sat in was an abandoned house in southeast Colorado. I was hunting with an outfitter buddy of mine by the name of Tom Tietz. Tom told me about a monster whitetail that he called "The Outhouse Buck" because twice the buck had been jumped near the old outhouse on the abandoned homestead.

"The attic of that old house would make a great stand for that buck," Tom said, "but so far none of my hunters will go in there."

"If that buck's as big as you say, I'd hang a stand in hell for a crack at him," I responded.

Tom dropped me off in the black of pre-dawn the next morning, told me to follow a certain fenceline for a quarter mile until it crossed a dry creek, and then to follow the creek north until I came to the long-abandoned ranch.

"With this wind, you should hear it before you see it," Tom said. "The old windmill has an eerie creak to it."

A half hour later I heard the rusted windmill complaining in the wind. Tom was right; it was eerie. But it was not nearly as eerie as stepping through the door of that long-abandoned ranch house.

Critters, mostly small, but one with larger claws — probably a raccoon — scampered everywhere when the beam of my little flashlight cast its weak glow over the abandoned living room. I swallowed hard and started up what was left of the stairs leading to the attic.

I'll admit I gave some thought to going back outside until it got light. But I fought back my apprehension, reminding myself that I was a grown man and that there was nothing to be afraid of in the old house. Somehow I made the top step and shined my light around the attic, which appeared to have been a bedroom, because the remains of a bed stood in one corner with a wooden kitchen chair.

An inch of bat "guano" covered the wooden floor, so the place smelled pretty ripe, and the air was probably less than healthy to breathe. As quietly as possible, which was not very quiet since the floor boards creaked and groaned with every cautious step, I set the chair by the north-facing window. Only one broken pane of glass remained in the window.

It took forever for day to break that morning. When it did, the bats began returning from their night of hunting. Trust me, Nancy and the girls would not have liked that, either. I did OK with the bats, but when a screech owl came swooping home through the window just over my head, it startled me so bad that I reared back and fell right off that wobbly, old chair.

When my heart started to beat again, I picked myself up off the floor and looked out the window just in time to see a white flag disappearing beyond the weed-choked remains of a corral.

It probably was not the Outhouse Buck, but then again, who knows?

Booner

The first time I ever saw the buck, he was picking his way along a brush-choked fenceline on an October morning. It was just breaking day, a jagged slash of pink creasing an otherwise sullen, gray sky. I was parked on a hill a quarter-mile away looking at him through the lens of my big spotting scope. Even at that distance, the buck took my breath away.

When he came within 100 yards of the road, I started the pickup and started down the road to intercept him. I wanted a closer look at this bruiser. My timing was perfect. The unconcerned buck stepped out on the road just as my pickup approached. He stopped in the middle of the road, looked at me as if to say, "You are on my road," then shifted into third gear and went over the alfalfa strips and into the timber on the ridge.

"What a magnificent creature," I said to myself.

Twice more that season the deer I nicknamed, "Booner" granted me a brief glimpse.

Once I saw

him from my stand as he walked the same fenceline where I had first seen him. Again, it was very early, well before dawn. Then that November, I saw him lumbering after a doe. During the winter and spring of 1999, the big buck crossed my mind often. Had he survived another year?

He had. When hunting season neared and I visited the folks who own the 160-acre Wisconsin farm where I hunt in the bluff country near Alma, they told me they'd seen the buck a few times during the summer. The buck did not live on the farm, only traveled through it on occasion, and I knew that my odds of catching that buck within bow range were slim, but each time out on the farm, I dreamed of having an up-close-and-personal meeting with "Booner."

That's what's so neat about knowing a monster buck cruises an area — you can always dream. For me, just knowing that Booner was somewhere around made it easier for me to pass up shots on other bucks that fall. In a lifetime of hunting white-tailed deer, I have seen only two other bucks of his caliber.

Then, one November afternoon, Booner and I met once again. I was sitting in a stand in a corner of woods that afforded me an unobstructed view of the ridge across the road where I suspected he bedded, since I'd seen him headed for that ridge two different times in the pink light of pre-dawn. Just after 4 p.m., I turned in my stand and scanned the alfalfa strip along the timber on that ridge.

There he stood in all his majesty, the low sun highlighting his tan coat and rich antlers. He was looking down into the valley. For a long time he just stared. Then, his mind made up, he loped across the open field for a third of a mile, crossed the county road, and disappeared from my view into one of the two small alfalfa fields on the farm.

I'd hunted that alfalfa field several times during the previous season, but had not seen much buck action, so I'd taken down the stand along the edge of the field. Bad mistake. That evening a whitetail party broke out in that field just out of my field of view. I considered climbing down and sneaking, but the odds of slipping within bow range of a whitetail are just slightly better than the odds of winning the lottery. Rattling provided better odds of pulling the buck in my direction so I beat my rattling antlers together hard for a couple of minutes, then waited.

When two button-buck fawns came running full tilt from the direction of the field, I knew some serious business was occurring in that strip of alfalfa since the youngsters had been asked to leave. The sun was sinking lower, and there I sat, 300 yards from a monster whitetail. I couldn't take it anymore. I climbed down and began skirting the edge of the timber hustling toward the strip of alfalfa.

It seemed light enough to easily see any deer in the field, but I was wrong. I was almost to the end of my cover when a doe lifted her tail, exposing the white underside. She was barely 60 yards away, and she was not alone. The big buck was pestering all of the does in the field to find a hot one. This hunter, meanwhile, knelt behind the last bit of cover as shooting light slowly seeped from the sky. Trying desperately to make something happen, I dug out the grunt call and imitated a buck tending a hot doe.

Booner didn't like competition. He left the does, but instead of coming across the field straight to me, he dropped into the finger of timber and came slowly toward me along the edge of the woods. He took his sweet time, and by the time the dark blob of his heavy body appeared just 10 steps away, it was too dark to shoot, even if there had not been a screen of cocklebur, blackberries, and brush between me and him. I sprawled out flat on my belly and hoped the buck would not discover me.

I got lucky. The buck stopped to destroy a hapless sapling, then busied himself pawing out a couple of bathtub-sized scrapes. When he dug that second scrape, the dirt from his flailing front hooves landed all around me.When he finished with his handiwork, he returned to his does. I resumed breathing, and in total darkness, snuck away, making a big loop back to my truck to ensure that I did not disturb the field.

The next day, Nov. 7, again was very warm, and I didn't think the buck would appear that evening. Still, I hung a stand in the corner of the alfalfa field near the scrapes of the previous evening and placed a single buck decoy 15 yards out in the alfalfa facing my stand. After placing four scent-soaked wicks in a circle around my stand, I climbed up and waited. The first trio of does and fawns entered the field before 4 p.m. A small buck followed, then another little 6-point. Each took turns half-heartedly chasing the does, then began munching the lush alfalfa.

The 6-point meandered down to my end of the field, spotted the decoy and ambled over. He approached in textbook fashion, circling downwind, then coming up nose-to-nose. The decent set of 8-point antlers on the decoy usually discourages small bucks, but the 6-point wanted to spar. He dropped his head, but received no response from the decoy. But when he jerked his head up, he caught the decoy under its plastic chin. The sound or feel of the plastic against his antlers made him jerk up all the harder, and he pulled the front two stakes that anchor the decoy out of the ground.

Now my decoy stood lopsided, but it didn't matter. In the next half hour, three more bucks approached the decoy. The last was a healthy 8-point, but with the big boy around, I did not even consider drawing. I had my heart set on one very special buck.

By sunset, the field was full of deer, 17 to be exact. When every deer in the field suddenly stopped and stared into a deep draw, I knew the big buck was coming. The big buck walked slowly through the field about 200 yards from my stand. It was too dark for him to see my decoy from that distance, so I gave a series of tending grunts followed by some doe bleats. He turned and approached. My right leg began to jump.

It had been a long time since I'd met a deer that made that leg jump the way it did when any deer approached. I hoped the buck wouldn't spot my one-legged jig up in the tree. After one last look at his antlers, I decided not to look at his rack again. Years ago I sent an arrow rattling around the rack of another big buck because my focus had been on horn instead of heart. That was not going to happen again.

Everything was perfect. Booner marched in just like the other bucks. He was head-on at 30 yards when it all unraveled. A small buck chased a doe out of the draw and under my stand. Booner turned on a dime and walked straight away from me. I drew and grunted. He stopped and looked back over his fat rump, but wouldn't turn. As he again walked away, I stopped him with another grunt. Again he looked back but offered no shot. That moment was the only time when I actually considered shooting a deer in the rump, but I did not and today, I'm glad that I passed.

The little buck saw the big boy and pulled up short. Booner postured, and the little buck tucked his tail and slunk away like a whipped dog. Booner turned his attention to the doe. At about 40 yards, he turned broadside and walked toward the doe. My arrow flew. The bright fletching was right on target but I had misjudged the range. The arrow sliced inches beneath his chest and landed harmlessly in the alfalfa. The big boy never even knew the arrow flew.

The next two days I hunted that alfalfa field from dark to dark both days, but Booner didn't appear. In fact, I saw few deer those two days, but temperatures in the 70s didn't help. On the last evening, I stopped by the home of the property owners to thank them for letting me hunt. When Mary opened the door, her first words were, "You got the big one, didn't you?"

"No," I said, "but I missed him on Sunday night."

"Oh," she said, " I was sure you had gotten him, because the last two evenings he has been right here in our yard chasing does, then this evening he did not show up."

"So that's where he disappeared to!" I said.

The rest of the story

I hunted hard for several more days during the remainder of the bow season, and while I saw many deer — including a respectable 8-pointer — Booner didn't reappear.

After an unsuccessful evening with no sign of him on Nov. 12, I stopped by the house just to let Joe and Mary know that I would not be back. Joe and Timmy were in the garage. We talked about the land, the deer, the flock of gobblers I'd seen and, of course, the big buck. Timmy, who was then in third grade, just listened as Joe and I rattled on about that deer. When I mentioned to Joe that I thought the big buck bedded on the high ridge across the road, Timmy simply said, "He comes out of the swamp."

"What makes you think so, Timmy?" I asked.

"Because when he comes through the yard chasing does, he is always wet and muddy," Timmy replied.

I thanked Joe and Timmy, got in the truck and headed back for Minnesota. Though I've hunted the property several times since then, I never saw Booner again, nor did I hear of any other hunters taking the big boy. To this day, my game of cat and mouse with Booner in late 1999 remains one of my most cherished hunting memories. He's still the biggest deer I've ever missed!

THE OFFSEASON

Spring scouting tips
Part 1: rubs

Because I write extensively about white-tailed deer hunting, conduct a number of seminars on deer hunting at some of the major "deer shows," and have the good fortune to spend more time hunting white-tailed deer than I ever dared dream, I've known and become friends with dozens of serious whitetail hunters.

These are guys (and a gal or two) who put a lot of time and effort into their whitetail hunting. That time and effort must be paying off, because this group of hunters take an impressive number of big bucks. They hunt in different parts of the country, use various types of equipment, and have their own preferred methods of hunting. But without exception, this group has one thing in common: All of them rely heavily upon spring scouting.

A good example of how important spring scouting is to the serious whitetail hunter is my friend Dave "Four-Wheeler" Haubrick. Dave lives in Pennsylvania but makes a trip to the Midwest to bowhunt for a week or two each fall. In early April, Dave takes a couple of his precious vacation days and drives to western Illinois to scout some land he and I hunt. What Dave learns on that April scouting trip pays off big in November.

The time to spring scout is during that two- or three-week period between snow melt and green up. Scouting while there is still snow on the ground is a waste of time because the snow covers most of the important sign. Once the trees sprout leaves and the grass is green, the best sign is more difficult to locate and follow.

Why scout in the spring? Good question. In the spring, you don't have to worry about disturbing deer like you do when scouting in the fall. Bump a deer now and it's no big deal. By the time the season opens, that deer will have forgotten all about your visit. The other reason why spring scouting is so valuable is that all of the sign from last November is right there in front of you. If you can read six-month-old sign, you are a giant step ahead of the hunter who waits until a week or so before opening day.

Rubs, scrapes, and trails are the three most important signs to look for in the spring. In the next three sections, let's take a look at these important points of spring scouting. We'll start with rubs.

Rubs

A mature buck will routinely rub trees as big around as your arm. Sometimes a smaller buck will add his scent to the big buck's rubs after the big buck has made it, but those big rubs are originally made by bucks with big antlers. A large buck does not rub exclusively on larger trees, but also will rub on smaller saplings, so don't ignore the smaller rubs. Key on the big ones; they indicate that you're on sign from a mature buck.

A single rub does not tell much of a story. A "rub line" on the other hand is like reading a big buck's diary. A mature buck will make rubs as he travels between his bedding and favored feeding areas. He will make rubs within the bedding area and along the edge of the fields or clear-cuts where he feeds. And when the testosterone begins to course through his veins, the buck will leave his mark on trees as he travels from one family group of does to the next searching for the scent of a doe in estrus. Rub lines divulge a buck's travel patterns — important information.

A rub in the spring is not as easy to spot as the same rub in the fall because time has dulled the sheen on the exposed inner layers. But find a rub or two and learn what to look for, and your eye will naturally be attracted to these six-month-old rubs.

Sometimes a rub line is as easy to follow as the hash marks down the middle of a highway, but don't count on it. Most of the time, ferreting out a rub line takes some detective work. Squat down and look in all directions when you find a big rub. Most of us look too high up on trees for rubs. Down low, your eye will more naturally be attracted to the next rub in sight. I always carry binoculars on my spring scouting excursions and often I've discovered the next rub in line not with the naked eye, but with the binoculars. If you can't see one, start hiking in the most likely direction you would expect to find the next rub. If you don't find one within 100 yards, turn around and try the other direction. If you try all directions and come up blank, write that rub off as an insignificant loner. You can see how following rub lines becomes a time-consuming endeavor.

Finding and following rub lines is not easy, but the rewards are worth the effort, because big bucks will make rubs along the same line this season, often using some of the same trees. One of the most encouraging signs you can find when reading rubs is a rub that shows the healed scarring of having been rubbed in previous years. And even if the buck that made the rub line has been killed, most of the time another good buck will take over the same route. A good rub line is like a prime sales territory in the business world; if one salesman gives it up, you can bet a half dozen others are waiting to move in on the vacated territory.

I can't tell you how close together the rubs in a rub line will be because they all vary. I've seen a few where you could squat down at a rub and easily see three or four more ahead of you. Sometimes though, it's 50 or more yards between rubs. About the time you're ready to give up, there will be another one.

I'm not convinced that the number of rubs is a good indicator of how often a buck travels a particular route. Research has shown that some bucks make more rubs than others, so just because rubs are sparse along a rub

Kneel and scan in all directions when searching for rub lines in the spring. Down low, your eye will more naturally detect the next rub.

line, don't assume that buck rarely travels that route. Just the opposite may be true.

Although I follow rub lines wherever they take me, the most important destination a rub line can lead me in my experience is to the buck's bedding area. The majority of those rubs you find are made at night. The bigger the buck, the more likely he is to post most of his signs under the cover of darkness. That's why a stand near the bedding area provides you with your best chance of either catching the buck vacating the bedding area in the evening or slipping back to the bedding area in the morning.

In my younger years I often made the mistake of hunting rub lines near food sources because this is often where rubs are most numerous. The problem, of course, is that most of these rubs are made at night. I would much rather hunt a skimpy rub line near the bedding area than a blazed trail near the food source.

And now for the bad news. There are places where you'll be hard-pressed to find a rub line made by a mature buck. This is because there are many areas where there are no mature bucks. If you do a thorough job of scouting your hunting area and come up with nothing but rubs on wimpy saplings, odds are excellent that there are no 3½-year-old bucks or older calling your hunting area home.

In the late '70s and early '80s I hunted just such an area. During all of the years, I saw one mature buck and a couple of his rub lines that spring. As my interest in hunting mature bucks grew, I abandoned those familiar haunts and sought areas where mature bucks were more numerous. When my search that spring led me to a big valley where rubs on ankle-thick trees were common, I went to work putting the pieces of the puzzle together. Rub lines were a big part of that puzzle.

Spring scouting tips
Part 2: scrapes

Now let's concentrate on scrapes. Many hunters lump rubs and scrapes together because they're frequently found near each other. But rubs and scrapes are two very different and distinct signs, and you should interpret them differently to get an accurate "read" on autumn deer activity in your hunting area.

Scrapes are not as easy to spot as rubs in the spring because they usually are obscured partially by leaves, twigs, branches, and forest duff. Don't expect that big, black oval-shaped patch of pawed-up earth that you frequently see in late October and November. In spring, a scrape is just a dull, leaf-littered bare spot that might easily be mistaken for a place where turkeys have scratched, if not for that tell-tale overhanging branch.

Over every scrape will be a branch where the buck — the one that made the scrape and any buck visiting it — will have deposited scent from its forehead, pre-orbital, saliva, and nasal glands. The branch usually will be about five feet off the ground. I've seen them as low as three feet and so high that deer had to stand on their hind legs to reach them. After some experience, the presence of the branch will most often attract you to the location of a scrape when scouting in the spring.

Scrapes are similar to rubs in that a single scrape means nothing while a string of scrapes, called a "scrape line" tells a pretty good story. Like rubs, bucks make scrapes along the routes they travel between bedding and feeding areas and as they roam their loosely defined home areas to find willing does. Like rubs, scrapes commonly show up along the same trails, edges, creek-bottoms, and ridge-lines.

But unlike a rub, where the size of the tree is a solid indicator of the status of the buck, the size of a scrape cannot be used to judge the maturity of the buck that made it. Most scrapes start out as oval-shaped pawings about the size of a laundry basket or slightly smaller. If a buck continues to use a scrape and works it at each visit, the scrape will become enlarged. When multiple bucks visit a scrape, that scrape can attain huge proportions. A scrape the size of your kitchen table, or a group of scrapes that touch and resemble a clover leaf, are not the work of a single buck, but rather a sign that multiple bucks are visiting the scrape.

Three or four different bucks may visit and add their scent to the same scrape. In areas with good buck densities, the number of bucks visiting a "community scrape" is remarkable.

One hunting buddy of mine once put a Cam-Trakker surveillance camera on a big scrape. In one night, all 24 exposures on the film were exposed. He had the film developed and upon inspection of the prints with a magnifying glass, he positively identified an astounding 21 different bucks that had visited that community scrape in a single night!

Scrapes in prime locations, like that community scrape in western Wisconsin, will appear in the same spot year after year. If the buck that originally made the scrape last season is killed, a new buck will continue the process this season.

Good scraping locations are never left vacant for long. I know of one old, abandoned homestead, deep in a valley of Minnesota's Whitewater Wildlife Management Area, where scrapes have been showing up in the same places for 20 years. As long as the overhanging branch is alive and reachable, bucks will continue to scrape in these prime locations.

In the spring, scrapes help me tie everything together. Scrapes provide clues to where a buck travels and where he searches for does. Like rubs, scrapes can lead me to bedding areas. Again, like rub lines, my favorite scrapes to hunt are those near, or sometimes even within, the buck's bedding area. These are the scrapes most likely to receive a visit during shooting light.

The number of scrapes in an area depends upon the competition between bucks for available does in that area. Scrapes will be most numerous in those areas that have both a decent buck-to-doe ratio and a fair percentage of mature bucks in the buck population. If the population is heavily swayed in favor of does, scraping activity is depressed.

Likewise, if there are few or no mature bucks in the population, scraping activity likewise will decrease. Mature bucks are not only the first to begin the scraping process each fall, but they're also the most productive in terms of the number of scrapes they paw out. If I scout an area in the spring and find few scrapes, I assume that I'm looking at an area with a high number of does compared to antlered bucks and an area that does not harbor many, if any, mature bucks. For me, this information alone is worth the time and effort I invest in spring scouting.

Spring scouting tips
Part 3: terrain

In the first section of this series, we looked at the importance of rubs. In the second column, we discussed scrapes. Both are important sign when scouting in the spring. Now we're going to look at how you can use deer trails and the terrain to bring it together to paint the entire picture.

But before I describe that, I should mention that I often scout deer in conjunction with spring turkey hunting. It's a perfect mix. In fact, I plan my spring turkey hunts around opportunities to scout places I hope to hunt in fall.

When scouting in the spring, I don't follow every deer trail. This would be too time consuming, given the number of trails criss-crossing most good deer habitat. Instead, I use the trails to help me tie together the buck rubs and scrapes I find. Many times the rubs and scrapes will be made along a trail, so it receives special attention. Very often this is the trail that will lead me to the buck's bedding area, and that's the trail I investigate.

Rarely will this trail be the most obvious one in the woods. Since mature bucks make their own trails, and since these trails are usually used only by a single animal, many would go overlooked if not for the presence of scrapes or rubs along them.

Does and fawns make the most heavily used trails. These family groups of three to sometimes seven or eight individuals make a lot of traffic. It's exciting when you find a deer trail that looks like a herd of Holsteins have been tromping along it every day for the past year, but if you're looking for a big buck, these obvious trails are rarely a good bet.

The reason: The mature bucks don't spend much time on these trails. In fact, about the only time a mature buck ventures onto these trails is when he happens to cut the trail of a hot doe during the rut or is in the company of a doe and follows her down the trail. Mature bucks may follow the same general path as the does and fawns, but they will almost always follow their own skinny, barely noticeable trail off to one side.

The trails I monitor first are buck trails leading to bedding areas, which you can identify by the rubs and scrapes along the trail. Second come trails winding through funnels. Third are trails crossing saddles. All deer often use the same trail to negotiate a funnel or to cross a saddle, which makes a stand along either one a good bet for seeing not only numbers of deer, but a good stand for taking a big buck, too.

When hiking the land in the spring, I note all the terrain features, but funnels and saddles are the most important. A funnel is any feature, either manmade or natural, that restricts the lateral movement of deer.

An hourglass is the classic shape. Where the hourglass narrows in the middle, that's the funnel. Examples to monitor are a skinny section of woods connecting two larger parcels, a place where a wooded creek bottom narrows or maybe a strip of woods pinched on one side by a harvested bean field and on the other by a river, highway, or another field.

Funnels are prime locations for a stand and are worth locating. Most funnels are obvious on an aerial photograph. Try to have one in hand before ever stepping foot on the property. They're worth every penny.

A saddle is a low spot in a steep ridge. Deer are no different than you and me. Whenever possible, they take the route of least resistance. This is how saddles become natural crossings for deer mov-

Always monitor fencelines during your spring scouting. Deer search for easy places to cross fences, and a well-used trail or even a chunk of hair provide clues to their presence.

ing from one side of a ridge to another. A stand overlooking a saddle in hill country such as you find in southeast Minnesota or southwest Wisconsin is hard to beat.

Speaking of deer taking the easy route, I always walk fence-lines when spring scouting. Deer can jump or slip through a fence anywhere, but they'll go out of their way to cross where the top strand is sagging. Same for deep ditches, creeks, or gullies. Deer will have specific places where they like to cross; these are the places you want a stand.

By the time I finish with my spring scouting I'll know where the water, food, and heaviest cover are located. I'll know how the trail system connects these places. I will have found every funnel, saddle, fence crossing, and creek crossing on the property, and I will have a good idea of the potential of the place for big bucks from the number and size of the rubs and the proliferation of scrapes. If I get real lucky I might even have picked up a shed antler or two.

Odds also are good that I'll have pruned a few shooting lanes and even have climbed a tree or two to prep it for hanging a stand in the fall. If I'm scouting on private land where I feel my stands are secure, I'll probably even hang a stand or two on my spring scouting mission. That's how confident I am that spring scouting can put me onto the perfect place for a stand.

Spring scouting is all about confidence. When I've scouted a place in the spring, I feel much more confident on the place when hunting season opens. I never feel that same confidence when going in "cold turkey."

By the time you read this final section of this three-piece collection on spring scouting, you should be prepared to hit the woods for what I consider to be the most important scouting of the year.

Getting the most from deer shows

If you're one of the thousands of people who attend the annual Minnesota Deer Classic, the deer expos in Wisconsin or Michigan, or another spring deer show around the country, here are some tips for getting the most out of the show.

• Few people attend deer shows alone. Getting together with buddies or family to go to such an event is an annual rite for many. The problem with groups (even a group of two) is that rarely will everyone in the group be interested in the same things. So staying together means that Joe sits through a seminar he's interested in; Pete, the non-bowhunter has to hang out while you and Joe look at the new archery equipment; then you and Joe are bored silly while Pete examines a new muzzleloader.

A better option? Pick a rendezvous point and time, then go your separate ways. A concession stand is my favorite meeting place. I can have a cold drink and one of those big pretzels while I wait.

Set more than one time to meet. "OK guys, let's meet here at the concession stand at noon, 2 p.m., and 4." That way you get to spend some time doing your own thing, but you also have the option of joining your buddies for part of the show.

•Build a schedule around the seminars. That may sound self-serving since I conduct seminars at shows (and would like to see you there), but I would offer the same advice even if it were Curt Wells and Shawn Perich up there on stage dishing it out.

The reason I build my show schedule around the seminars is that's what draws me to a show. If not for the opportunity to learn more about whatever the seminar subject happens to be, I would not bother attending any sport show. I've never been to a good seminar where I did not learn something.

Often at shows I have people approach me and say they really wanted to hear my seminar but just couldn't get there. A little advance planning goes a long way in accomplishing all of your goals at a show.

•White-tailed deer-oriented consumer shows are good places to begin researching hunts. Say you and your buddies are thinking about a spring black bear hunt in Canada. Peruse the program and highlight the Canadian outfitters. Spend some time with each.

Researching at the show allows you to meet the outfitter personally. If you're any judge of human character, you can usually get a pretty good feel for a person when you have a chance to talk with him for a while. That's harder on the phone or the Internet. Take one of the brochures; if it does not include the names and numbers of a half dozen or more references, ask for them. If an outfitter hedges at providing references, there's a reason.

Many outfitters will run a "special show price" as an incentive for booking a hunt at the show. Personally, I would never book a hunt without contacting as many references as possible first, so I won't book a hunt at the show. However, if I'm interested in a certain outfitter, I will tell him that I'm going to check with a few references and that I will make my decision within a week, two weeks, or by a certain date. Then I ask if the special show price will still apply. I've never been told no yet.

And then there are the deer — row after row of impressive mounts. Most show-goers simply stroll through the aisles admiring the mounted heads, and that's the way it should be. However, if you're interested in field-judging bucks, there is no better place than at a deer show.

With a notepad and pen in hand, I walk down an aisle, glance at each deer head and write what I believe the antlers will score. When I've finished an aisle, I go back through and check my estimates against the actual score sheets. When I began this exercise, my tally usually came within 15 to 20 inches of the actual score. Now I'm down to about five.

THE OFFSEASON

Spring hunting
for sheds

I spend so much time hunting white-tailed deer, many people assume that I hunt for shed antlers, but that is not the case. Oh, I've found some sheds over the years, but mostly by accident. One time, while turkey hunting, I actually sat on what remained from a rodent-chewed shed.

To be honest, shed hunting's not my bag. It's great when I stumble across a shed, but it's not like my heart races and my palms get all sweaty. The only sheds that really trip my trigger are the sheds I find while spring scouting areas I intend to hunt in the fall. Those sheds are proof that the buck made it through the hunting season. Unless that buck dies of natural causes, he should be around come opening day. That excites me.

But I've got buddies who are really into hunting shed antlers. One of them is Tom Indrebo, who with his wife, Laurie, runs Bluff Country Outfitters in Buffalo County, Wis. Tom has piles of shed antlers that he, Laurie, and their son, Shane, have found.

Of all of the seriously affected whitetail junkies I know, Tom is the most hopeless whitetail addict. His farm is kind of like "whitetail central." Hunters are always stopping in to show Tom the deer they took during the fall or the sheds they find in the spring. So I turned to him for some tips on when, where, and how to find shed antlers.

The first question I put to him was timing: Is early spring a good time to look for sheds, or is it too late?

"That's a fine time for locating sheds," Tom said. "The snow has just melted, but the grass is not high enough to cover the sheds yet, and farmers have not worked up the fields. Once the grass and underbrush are lush and farmers have worked the fields to plant their crops, finding sheds becomes real tough."

161

For many shed hunters, early spring is their favorite time to look for antlers. Others prefer winter. In the winter, the shed antlers will sometimes lie on top of the snow, especially a crusted snow. They are easy to see then, because often they are the only thing sticking up above the snow. But if the snow is soft, a heavy antler will drop down into it and be difficult to find.

"Also, when you have a winter where a lot of snow drops every few days during the time when the bucks are dropping their antlers, that fresh snow will cover them up. In the spring, when the snow melts, all of those sheds, which have been buried, become visible, so shed hunters can hit a real bonanza in the spring."

A field where deer fed during the winter provides the most logical place to begin your search for sheds, Indrebo says. The longer the deer fed in the field, the better your odds of finding numbers of dropped antlers. The more concentrated the deer, the better your odds, too.

Lots of people feed deer these days, and they find a lot of sheds near their feeding stations or in their food plots. In a tough winter, deer are hard-pressed for food, and a hungry deer is not shy about feeding on a farmer's bales, silage piles, or spilled grain around grain bins. If you saw deer around places like this during the winter, go back to those places and ask the landowner if you can look for sheds.

"A shed antler is pretty easy to spot in the spring if it is lying in bean stubble or an alfalfa field, but cornfields are another story. An antler blends right in with cornstalks, and if I know that it is a good field where deer fed heavily during the winter, I'll walk every row to make sure that I do not overlook any sheds. If the cornstalks have been chopped, it's a little easier, because the antlers, at least a good one, will stick up higher than the mulched stalks, but a cornfield that has been picked, but not chopped, or a standing field demands real diligence to locate all of the sheds."

Fields are the easiest places to find sheds, but Indrebo also finds them along trails. When deer are feeding heavily on one food source in the winter, they have some very well-defined trails. He hikes these paths, keeping an eye on the trail and just off to each side.

"Lots of times these trails will lead me to bedding areas,

which always are worth investigating. In the bluff country like we have here in western Wisconsin, southeast Minnesota, and northeast Iowa, deer spend a lot of time on points in the winter, especially those with a southern exposure where they can take advantage of the winter sun," he said.

Driving around in the winter, Indrebo takes note of the points where he sees deer and returns to those places in the spring to search for sheds. Deer spend a lot of time in these places, so it's almost always worth the effort to hike in for a look around, he says.

"Of course, shed hunters are not the only ones interested in those fallen antlers. Squirrels and other critters love to chew on sheds, and it seems that the worse the winter, the more inclined they are to gnaw on antlers.

"I'm always amazed at just how quickly a squirrel can clean up a shed antler. Give a single squirrel just four or five days and he will have all of the points gnawed off a nice shed. That's why, the quicker you can start searching once the snow is melted, the better your odds of finding antlers that have not been chewed up. I'm afraid squirrels are better shed hunters than we will ever be," Tom said.

But I had one more question for Tom. How do you develop an eye for sheds? A mutual friend of ours, Pat Reeve, who lives in Plainview, Minn., can be traveling down the road at 65 miles per and spot a shed antler 75 yards off the road in a field. Others, like me, pretty much have to step on one.

"It's hard to explain,"

Tom Indrebo, of Buffalo County, Wis., spends time every spring walking the bluff country in search of shed antlers. The location and size of sheds can provide insight into buck activity and local deer habits and behavior.

Indrebo said. "For me it's like I look at an area and I find the place where the deer fed during the winter and the trail or trails they used to get to the feeding area, and I'll get this feeling like this is the spot to look. Sometimes I'll look down and there will be a shed antler. I don't think it's so much the fact that one shed hunter has better eyesight than the other or some uncanny knack for spotting antlers."

In short, spotting sheds is something developed over time. The more sheds you find, the easier they are to spot.

For Tom Indrebo and others like him, searching for shed antlers is just another phase of the hunt. Many times while visiting at Tom's place, he'll show me a shed antler and then show me some video he has shot of that buck or maybe a photo taken with one of his many surveillance cameras. It's not uncommon for Tom to find a shed or sometimes the highly coveted "matched set," then have one of his hunters take that same buck in the fall.

To Tom and many like him, the sheds are trophies themselves, but more importantly, they are a piece of the whitetail puzzle.

Pre-season hunting preparation

One early autumn evening I was in the backyard sitting in a treestand hanging a few feet off the ground, dressed in a Heater Body Suit, plunking arrows into targets. The Heater Body Suit is the ultimate in cold weather clothing. It was 85 degrees and sticky outside. My neighbor, who considers me his main source of entertainment, hollered over and suggested I had better wear a stocking cap before frostbite struck.

Nancy Clancy, sitting in the shade on the deck sipping ice water, chuckled. I just ignored them and kept shooting. Non-hunters will never understand the importance of pre-season preparations, but it always amazes me how many hunters ignore this step. Most missed opportunities are not the result of a major flaw, but rather because of the "little things."

If I had $5 for every sob story I've heard about the deer that got away because a stand creaked at the wrong time, a rangefinder malfunctioned, the bowstring snagged loose clothing, caught a facemask, or snagged the lanyard of a grunt call or a binocular strap, I'd be packing a hefty roll.

Eliminate the "little things," and your odds of success instead of a sob story escalate dramatically.

So I dress in a Heater Body Suit in 80-degree weather. I know that I can slip the suit from my shoulders, draw my bow and shoot without the string making contact with the suit. I can do it while seated and while standing. By the time I finish these short (but sweaty) summer sessions, I know that no matter which direction I need to shoot, I can do it.

Often I wear a turkey vest while bowhunting. With the multitude of pockets, I've found them perfect for carrying the small items. Grunt call in this pocket, rattling bag on the left, rangefinder on the right, candy bars everywhere. Since I sometimes wear the turkey vest on stand, I practice while wearing it in my backyard. You don't want some string snagging on one of those pockets bulging with Snickers! I'll shoot with the same gloves I'll be wearing, the same face masks, and the same caps. Too extreme? I don't think so.

Shooting from a treestand strapped a couple feet off the ground to a backyard ash means I can see if my stands creak or squeak when I shift my weight. Then I know they are rock solid even when I stand on the edge, lean out on my safety harness, and make an awkward shot. Now's the time to learn these things.

Using each of my treestands in my practice sessions provides an opportunity to safety inspect each stand, and I refresh my memory on how to hang the stands. I have stands from several manufacturers, and each is a little different. Securing them to a tree in my backyard a time or two ensures that when I hang one in the deer woods, even in the dark, the operation will go quickly, smoothly, and quietly. My neighbors think I've gone off the deep end when I walk each of my climbing stands up and down the telephone pole a couple of times, but it pays dividends in the deer woods.

Along about this time of year, I spend some time sorting the gear in my turkey vest or day pack. There are two pull-up ropes, a couple of spare screw-in bow hangers, rangefinder, small binoculars, two Tru-Talkers, a rattling bag, a spare release, extra gloves and face mask, dry socks, a pruning shears, small saw, pocket knife, field dressing gloves, a couple of squeeze bottles of wind checker, assorted scents and wicks, a small camera,

A pre-season gear check, even in summer's heat, will boost your bowhunting "luck factor."

small flashlight with extra batteries, a bottle of scent spray and one of powder, flagging, a tube or waterproof matches and a cube of fire-starter just in case, a Bug-Out headnet for those early season skeeters and a Zip-Loc bag with a half dozen of those chemical handwarmers. T.P. goes in another Zip-Loc, and a third serves as my first-aid kit, containing Tylenol, eye drops, cough supprescent, Band-aids and a small whistle.

Seems like a lot of stuff for a kid who started with a Herter's recurve, three arrows, and a Case knife with one of the blades snapped off, but I've used it all, and with this assortment of gear I can spend a full day on stand or survive a night in the woods.

The bow is the one piece of equipment on which most hunters lavish some pre-season attention. In case you have not, here are some important points.

•Check that string. If it shows sign of wear, don't be cheap, install a new one.

•Tighten all of the screws and bolts, then go back and tighten them again.

•If you practice all summer with target points, don't just assume that your broadheads will shoot the same. Most don't. And yes, that includes mechanical heads.

Late summer scouting

By about mid August every year, we bowhunters get a little antsy.

Sure it's still summer, but hey, our opening day is less than a month away. The first tolerably cool evening finds many of us headed out to a favorite deer woods to scout a little. We slash our way through the thick foliage, swatting mosquitoes, seeing nothing, and spreading our scent throughout the place we want to hunt. That's bad business when it comes to white-tailed deer, especially mature bucks.

I'm no different than the rest of you. By August my bow is tuned, the broadhead-tipped arrows are finding their mark on my backyard targets with satisfying frequency, and my neighbors are chuckling as I test stands on backyard trees. But I don't go wandering around the deer woods at this time of the year.

My scouting still occurs. Many evenings this month will find me snooping around the places I'll hunt this fall, but most of the time I don't even get out of my pickup truck. No, I'm not lazy; when it comes to hunting, I'll work as hard as anyone. But I can discover a whole lot more about deer in my hunting country, come September, if I stay out of the woods in August.

Most of the time, scouting means looking for sign like trails, rubs, scrapes, tracks, and droppings. But not now. Now you look for the deer themselves. That's the best sign.

The white-tailed deer is a spooky, nervous critter. Mature deer border on paranoia. But in late summer, even big deer are as relaxed as you'll ever see them. It's been seven months since anyone hunted them. Their guard is down. A summer of easy living has made them fat, sleek, and lazy.

In the agricultural regions of the Midwest, the deer will feed in soybean or alfalfa fields each evening. They're very visible, which makes for easy spotting. In the forested north, where clear-cuts and natural meadows attract deer, spotting deer is more difficult, but still as easy as it ever gets.

The neat thing about locating deer at this time of the summer is that the deer you see feeding in a field this evening probably will be there again tomorrow (and the next day) unless the food source undergoes a dramatic change. Unless those beans are harvested or nipped by a hard frost, that same deer likely will be right there on opener. When it comes to patterning a specific buck, this is your best chance of the season.

I like to watch deer on enough evenings to know they are committed to one field. Once I know that they're not "hopscotching" from field to field, common where good fields are abundant, I arrive earlier each evening so I can see where the deer are exiting the cover.

Deer usually won't randomly enter a field; instead they have specific locations. It might be a place where the fence is lower so they can easily hop over it or slide between the strands. It might be an open gate, a gully, or a finger of brush jutting into the field. Watch the deer enter the field on a few evenings, and you can pinpoint these spots. Draw a map and use a landmark, like a tall tree, a branch drooping out over the field, or maybe a radio tower or a notch in a ridge, to find the entry point with a minimum of tromping around. Then look for more deer on another field and repeat the process.

On fields that I can't see from the road, I use a high vantage point to provide a view of the field, even if that vantage point is a half

Your scouting tactics during those final, jittery days before archery season opens can make or break your early season hunting success.
Photo by John D. LaMere

169

mile away. With a good pair of binoculars and a spotting scope, distance is no problem. I've used stacks of hay bales, silos, barns, rocky outcroppings, and have climbed a lot of trees in the heat of summer to snoop. More than once, I've gotten a friend with a plane to fly me over these hidden fields at prime time. (Offer to pay for the fuel, and guys with planes are more than happy to take you for a ride. They're always looking for an excuse to fly.)

By doing this several evenings a week, usually by the first week in September. I'll have found a buck or two and will have secured permission to hunt the land.

I check on the deer a week before the season to make sure they're still using the field and the entry point, then I go in sometime between mid-morning and mid-afternoon when I know deer will be tucked away in their bedding area. I find the entry point and hang my stand. I'll spend as little time as possible at the site, cut a few shooting lanes, then get out and won't return until hunting time.

This system is as close to fool-proof for early season deer as you can get unless.... For more on the "unless," reread the appetizer chapter on Page 43 in the second section of this fabulous tome.

After your deer is down

People who know that I hunt deer often assume that I always get one, so they'll ask me what I do with all of the meat. Those who know me will never ask!

Seriously, my answer is that none goes to waste. Whether I fly to a distant destination or am hunting out my back door, I either make arrangements to give the meat to someone who really wants it, or my family eats it. When all three of the Clancy girls were living at home, our family ate three to six deer each year. Of course there were always a couple of neighbor kids sitting at our table to help. Half of the kids in Byron, Minn., have been introduced to wild game around the Clancy table. Looking back over all of those years, I cannot recall a single time when one of those children did not enjoy their meal of venison. Many of them looked forward to it. "What's for dinner, Mr. Clancy?" one of the urchins would ask.

"Clancy's Baked Venison Round Steak Special," I would exclaim, using the fancy name for one of my favorite recipes.

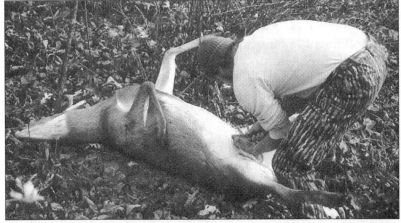

Congratulations on successfully harvesting your deer, but you're only halfway to tasty venison tablefare. Your actions after your deer is down are important, too.

"Oh, good," the urchin would exclaim, then rush off to spread the word among the other kids.

Yet, I know many hunters and their families who don't like venison. Some hunters will throw away last year's packaged meat before going hunting this year. And yet, in fancy restaurants out East and especially in Europe, venison is on the menu. High-rollers pay big bucks for the same meat many of us ignore. What gives?

As I see it, there are three steps to good venison. Proper care in the field, proper butchering, and of course, the cooking. Botch any of the three and you're in for an undesirable table experience.

In the field

It begins with shot placement. A shot through the lungs, via bullet or broadhead, kills quickly and ruins little meat. After taking some nice photos, gut the deer. I'm always amazed at the size of knives some deer hunters wear on their belts. A pocket knife is ideal for deer. I like one with a 3-inch blade. First I pull on a pair of rubber field dressing gloves. Using a long, thin blade, cut around the anus. Now slice through the skin but not into the cavity from the anus to the brisket.

On the next cut, insert the knife just under the membrane, and if you're right-handed, use the trigger finger and middle finger of your left hand as a guide for the knife blade, pushing down with your left hand so that you won't cut through the stomach. Slice through the diaphragm, reach up (this is where the above-the-elbow gloves pay off) and cut the windpipe. Pull hard and everything will come out.

Cut off the plumbing and pull out the rest from the rear where you made the cut around the anus. Some hunters like to split the pelvic bone, but I do not. When you drag a deer out they'll sometimes flop onto their bellies when you drag them over a log and if you have split the pelvic bone, the deer will be spread-eagled and collecting dirt and debris on the hindquarters.

Hang the deer from the head when you get home.

Butchering

Whether you butcher it yourself or use a processor, you should end up with meat free of debris, hair, and foreign matter. Nothing will turn off the cook quicker than unwrapping the night's main course and finding any of the above. Strong flavor in venison comes from fat and bone.

The only fat you'll find on venison will be a layer on the back and rump. A buck taken after the rut may have converted all of this fat to energy during the rut. I've seen bucks without a speck of fat on them, which is why some of the big boys do not make it through a severe winter. Bone the meat; do not use a meat saw. Take the time to remove all of the connective tissue (sometimes called silver skin) between layers of meat.

Instead of cutting up individual steaks, I leave the meat in one chunk, then cut it when I thaw the meat. Double wrap everything to protect against freezer burn.

Cooking

When our oldest daughter, Michelle, went to college, I was tickled one day when she called home to say she was catching a ride with a friend and would be home for the weekend. "Oh and Dad," she said before she hung up, "could we have venison backstrap on the grill when I get home?" I knew I had done something right.

There's no one definitive tip to preparing venison that you, your family, and friends will look forward to again and again. But there are dozens and dozens of secrets. These "secrets" are found in recipes in wild game cookbooks. Some are simple, some demand a little more work. Try them. Find the ones you and your family enjoy the most. But even then, keep on experimenting with new recipes. That's how you keep venison a favorite instead of an "Oh ish!" with your family. Here are two of our family's favorite recipes for venison. Try them this year at your home.

Backstraps on the grill

This is about as simple, yet tasty, as they come. When butchering your deer, have the backstraps cut into chunks, but not steaked out. It takes a chunk 12 to 15 inches long for a hungry family of five. Roll the meat in your favorite seasoning. I like Lawry's, but there are other excellent varieties, or you can simply use salt and pepper. Lay the meat directly on the grate over the coals. If you like, baste the meat with BBQ sauce. Cook until it's pink in the middle. Have everyone at the table and ready to eat when you bring it in because venison is best served very hot. I leave mine on a cutting board and slice it to order.

Those who like it well done get end cuts. I like mine pink, so my cuts come from the center. Tender, delicious, and easy.

Clancy's "Deceiver" Venison Round Steak

I call this one "The Deceiver" because whether I use deer, moose, elk, caribou or antelope, even the fussiest eaters just figure they're dining on beef. Of course I never tell them the truth until we're finished eating.

•Cut round steaks 1-inch thick and pound with a mallet to tenderize.

•Roll the pounded steaks in seasoned flour.

•Brown in butter or oil at medium heat.

•Place steaks in a baking pan.

•On top of each steak add one teaspoon of brown sugar, a teaspoon of catsup and a teaspoon of butter. Sprinkle each steak with chopped onion.

•Add a ¼ cup of venison or beef stock to the frying pan and scrape all of the drippings loose and pour this in the baking dish with the steaks.

•Cover the pan with aluminum foil. Bake at 350 for 45 minutes and then uncover and bake for another 15 minutes.

•I put potatoes and a squash in the oven at the same time so I can pull the whole meal out of the oven at once. Enjoy.

Observations

•Over the years I've often heard that venison from northern forests doesn't taste as good as venison from ag country. This seems to make sense, since the deer in the agricultural regions have access to corn, soybeans, alfalfa, and other succulent crops, while their northern cousins live mainly on browse and grass. But I've eaten deer from all regions of our state and from a dozen other states and Canadian provinces. Guess what? Whitetails taste like whitetails no matter where they live or eat.

• There are those who believe that "aging" meat — letting the deer hang — makes it more tender and better tasting. Others say just the opposite. I've had it both ways, and I taste no difference.

•During basic training at Ft. Campbell, Ky., and then AIT at Ft. Polk, La., back in the late 1960s, I discovered the sad truth that in the right hands (such as those of a U.S. Army cook) the best cut of meat in the world can be rendered inedible. Most bad venison is not the fault of the deer, but rather the cook.

Enjoy your white-tailed deer hunting ... and your white-tailed deer eating, too. You've earned it!